T0149426

A GHOST OF CHE

A Motorcycle Ride Through Space, Time, Life and Love

Mauktik Kulkarni

iUniverse, Inc.
New York   Bloomington

Dedicated to:
My family, for giving me the ability to write
and a girl, for giving me the inspiration to write

Contents

PREFACE

They say that every life is a book. It's just sitting at the bottom of a deep ocean called *The Writer's Block*. It takes a lot of inspiration to take the plunge and a lot of hard work to dig that book out. For some, inspiration comes in the form of a life-changing event that makes them throw themselves off a cliff and into the ocean. For others, it comes in the form of a series of unique and quirky experiences as they walk through their lives. The happiness, sympathy, sadness, ecstasy, or loneliness evoked by those experiences makes them dip their toes in the ocean. And before they know it, they are racing to the bottom of the ocean.

In my case, the inspiration was a bit of both. The idea of writing a book was never really strange or unusual to me. As a kid growing up in a small town in India, I always knew that I would write a book about something. While there was nothing particularly interesting about my Indian middle-class childhood, writing was like eating, sleeping, and breathing. Sooner or later, it was going to happen.

The inspiration started trickling in when I left my hometown. Looking back, I don't think there was any elaborate plan to find inspiration. It was not a result of a creative writing course. If anything, I spent four years of college writing, and sometimes copying, the dry technical documents and reports. Neither was it a culmination of some long reading spree. Other than textbooks and scientific journals, my reading experience is limited to less than fifty books. It's just the standard stuff: a few mystery novels, few biographies, few travelogues, and a few history books. No Shakespeare. No Mark Twain. No Jane Austen. No Aristotle. No Plato. No Kant. No Chomsky. Rather, the inspiration came from moving to a big city for college. Standing on my own feet. Setting goals for myself. Motivating myself. Becoming independent.

Then came the culture shock of moving to the United States. As a typical Indian immigrant on my way to become overeducated, I thought a PhD was a panacea. I thought I would have a good job, a stable career, and all that jazz. But the graduate school experience turned out to be an eye-opener for me, in more ways than one. Neuroscience started opening my mind's eye to the reality of my own mind—my behavior, my habits, my feelings, and my perception of the world around me. It was interesting to learn how that small little organ called the brain helps us accomplish these seemingly trivial, yet amazing, feats. It gave me a whole new paradigm to understand and relate to the life around me.

My clashes with American culture led to a sea change in my middle-class Indian mentality. Meeting people from all over the world gave me the opportunity to appreciate their ways of life. Throwing myself off the cliff by falling in love with a virtual stranger made me question my own beliefs. And a freak sports injury brought me face to face with the reality that life is too short. After breaking my arm in an otherwise uneventful football (or soccer) game, I found myself lying in a hospital bed, contemplating surgery. The surgeon walked in a few minutes before the surgery and started briefing me about the planned intervention. It was a routine surgery. But, having spent my childhood in India, I had a mental image of a doctor as a compassionate guy trying to comfort you and relieve your anxieties—not someone reading you a patients' bill of rights! So, when I saw his wooden face and heard his expressionless voice saying, "There is a 1–2 percent chance of death under general anesthesia," it was a rude awakening for me. The checklist was ready when I woke up after the surgery: love, a motorcycle ride thought South America, and a book.

Love has turned out to be a bittersweet experience. There's nothing unusual about it. I have decided to hang a Work in Progress sign on the front door and made my peace with it. My solo motorcycle ride through South America, inspired by *The Motorcycle Diaries*, was a great success. What started out as a lonely ride through the back roads of Peru slowly turned into a cautious embrace of the culture of South America. My encounters with a Chilean bike mechanic, a struggling Argentinean artist, a Brazilian free spirit, a Belgian cross-country cyclist, a German social worker, and a bunch of generous Peruvians opened my eyes to a completely new reality of life. The trip gave me a chance to take a time-out from my old life and experience a new life. It helped me take a step back, appreciate what I had, and forget about what I did not have.

My solo motorcycle ride through South America also gave me a chance to contemplate the legacy of Che Guevara. More than four decades after his assassination, all the ideologies have crumbled under their own weight. Soviet communism, European socialism, and American capitalism have all shown their strengths and weaknesses, leaving all the other countries to chart their own courses toward salvation. Nonetheless, even in this era of national individualism, love and compassion seem to be the key ingredients for global social and economic development. My trip gave me an opportunity to renew that human bond of love and compassion. All in all, it was a beautiful trip. I had the time of my life!

I came back to the United States armed with some five hundred pictures from the trip. For someone who had never owned a camera and does not fancy going through other people's pictures, five hundred pictures was a huge burden. Writing a book to accompany the pictures just made sense. After torturing my uncle and aunt with those pictures, I expressed my desire to write a book about my trip. My aunt jumped on the idea.

My move to Louisville to join a small start-up company gave me the much-needed solitude to write a book. I had a new job, a new city, no roommates, and no friends. It was time for the rubber to hit the road—rather, it was time for the fingers to hit the keypad. There was only one problem. I had been a social animal all my life, and it was impossible to imagine a life without friends. Wasting my evenings sitting in front of a computer was a scary thought. But that's when my aunt's constant encouragement, prodding, and follow-ups saved the day. Her relentlessness helped me wade through the rough waters of *The Writer's Block* and get to the bottom of the ocean. When the first draft was ready, my friend Paul Fitzgerald was kind enough to review it and give his comments. As he was a published author and a non-family member, his encouragement made me think seriously about publishing it.

This book is a product of the countless hours spent staring at a blank computer screen without writing a single word. Motorcycle ride? Checked. Writing a book? Checked. Back to love.

ONE:
Start Your Engines

Tornado warnings. Severe weather warnings. Sirens. I was preparing for another delayed or canceled flight, another chapter in my love/hate relationship with airlines and airports. As much as I hate them, the airlines and airports love to have me over. A standard two-hour domestic flight turns into an all-night-long affair when I am on board. And this was an international flight. My itinerary had stops in Atlanta and Lima. *No delays, please!*

I dumped my backpack in the trunk, picked up Lonely Planet's *South America on a Shoestring* and *English-Spanish*

1

Phrase Book from a local bookstore, and got to the airport. The short good-bye phone calls to two buddies turned into half-hour conversations. "I hope you die somewhere in South America and never come back," one of my buddies said. It got me thinking about the mission I was on. After all, I had been waiting for this day for three years. Even the director of *The Motorcycle Diaries* must have said "Damn, I wanna be that guy riding the motorcycle!" after the first screening of the movie.

Three countries in forty days. Armed with a tent, a sleeping bag, five shirts, two pairs of jeans, a jacket, fifteen power bars, a jar of Gatorade powder, a bottle of water, a cell phone, two credit cards, my passport, and sign language, I reached the airport. For a change, the flight was not delayed. *Way to go!* I fastened the seatbelt and opened the Peru section in my Lonely Planet guide. It was my first trip to South America. I had no experience riding or fixing 400-cc motorcycles. My Spanish vocabulary consisted of ten words. A Chilean friend had repeatedly warned about the muggings, robberies, and lootings in South American countries. I'd learned that I was about to cross the driest desert on earth. I wouldn't have been surprised if I hadn't come back. But how many times do you get an opportunity like this?—no family obligations, no pending bills, a secure future. I was ready for the trial by fire.

I had planned the first two days of my trip, Cuzco to Puno, and Puno to Moquegua or Tacna. That was it. I had a motorcycle, a tent, and a sleeping bag for emergency. NOT having a plan was my plan. I just wanted the road to lead me.

I thought about calling my brother from the Atlanta airport, but decided against it. I stuck to the original script, telling my family about my plan after I reached Peru. It was close to midnight when I reached Lima. I slept in the waiting room at the Lima airport and got on board the first flight from Lima to Cuzco. It was five in the morning.

I was in Cuzco by 6:30. Two guys from the motorcycle rental agency were at the airport to pick me up. We rode back to the rental agency on 250-cc motorcycles. I was riding a motorcycle after almost three years. And it was reassuring to find out that our brains don't forget motorcycle-riding skills.

The rental agency was in the heart of the city, near the Plaza de Armas. I filled out the paperwork and handed it over. I was waiting for the rental agency guy to get back from the notary's office and hand me the border-crossing papers. In came the first piece of bad news! There was some kind of statewide strike in the Cuzco region.

If I understood it right, and that was a big *if*, the Peruvian government had proposed to allow travel agents from Lima to book tours to Machu Picchu. The agents in the Cuzco region were obviously not happy with that. They figured the Lima agents were going to steal their business now. So they decided to express their anger by blocking all roads out of Cuzco. They even forced all the government offices to close down. There was no way of getting the papers notarized that day. It didn't sound like a very good start.

The strike had shut the entire city down. All I could do that day was take pictures of the angry Cuzco*ites* and visit a nearby site called *Saqsayhuamán*, the site of the last battle between the Spanish and the Incans. It's a beautiful site with walls of carefully crafted stones. It's true that nothing, not even air, can pass through the gaps between two stones. The imposing walls, the hallways lined with well-crafted doors, the underground passageways—it's impressive for a five to six-hundred-year-old structure. And just when the intricate web of walls, hallways, doors, and stairs starts getting monotonous, one of the doors shows you the entire valley of Cuzco.

It's an enormous city that was destroyed during the Spanish conquest. The Peruvians have rebuilt it. But it feels like it was rebuilt without any serious planning. It's just blocks and blocks of concrete jungle dotted with grand old plazas. Lost in the suffocating concrete, you can almost hear the ancient plazas screaming, "Don't touch me!"

As I started riding around town, I realized that most of the other roads were barricaded. I spent some time at the central plaza and went back to the rental agency. The young boy at the agency volunteered to walk me to a nearby *hostal barato*. As we were walking down, he started asking me all kinds of questions in *Español*. I opened the *Español-Inglés* translation section in my phrase book and handed it over to him. He just wanted to know the basics: my nationality, my age, my job. Nationality and age were easy. I had read that on the flight. But my job? How do you say *Neuroscience* in Spanish? My efforts lasted for about a minute, or two, maybe. I guess *estudiante* was good enough for him.

He was keen on learning English, and I wanted to learn how to ask simple questions in *Español*. So I started asking him questions about what he did, whether he went to college, and how to ask those questions in *Español*. He gave me the translations and started talking about himself. He told me that he could survive with the money he was making by fixing motorcycles, manning the desk, and helping the tourists out. A college degree wasn't all that important to him. Was he really happy with what he was doing? Was he forced to work there out of financial compulsions? I wish I knew *Español*!

He left me at the hostel and disappeared in the small alleys of Cuzco. I unpacked, took a shower, and started cramming Spanish words into my non-cooperating brain. It had been a long journey. And the seats at the Lima airport were seats, not futons or beds. I wanted to take a nap, but my adrenalin was not going to let me do that. Millions of thoughts were racing through my mind. Every day was going to be a new adventure. I had no idea what to expect. Language was going to be a liability. My five, or maybe even six, senses were going to be more important than my ability to speak. It was going to be fun!

I gave up on my pathetic attempts at falling asleep. It was time for dinner, anyway. I walked into a nearby restaurant and asked the girl about Peruvian delicacies. "Guinea pig," she said emphatically. The thought of eating a guinea pig made me uncomfortable. I had no intention of killing another one of those poor little souls. I had spent almost every day of my past year waking up and apologizing to those lab rats before sacrificing them for the sake of science. As a graduate student, you gotta do what you gotta do. But I didn't want to kill another guinea pig for my dinner. Then again, why didn't I feel uncomfortable ordering chicken?

*   *   *

With the notary taking his own time to sign my border-crossing papers, I had to wait until eleven o'clock the next day to leave Cuzco. I reached Puno just before five o'clock in the evening. Moquegua was another two hundred kilometers. The summer days were long, with sunlight until eight or eight-thirty. My average speed was seventy to eighty kilometers per hour. It would be possible to get to Moquegua before dark. I filled my thirsty tank up and decided to press on. One wrong turn and, within a couple of hours, I was on a dirt road. Another half an hour and darkness joined the empty dirt road. Another fifteen minutes and the stream running across the road made me use my brakes. I could almost hear the stream laughing at me as I fought to keep the bike from falling down.

I was in the middle of the Andes, at twelve to thirteen thousand feet above sea level, on a cold night—with an empty dirt road, no street lights, and a heavy motorcycle made heavier by my backpack staring at me. What was I to do? I was clueless—dazed and confused. After waiting for ten to fifteen minutes, I was preparing to camp out on the roadside. Luckily, the Peruvians had some other plans for me.

A set of headlights broke the darkness. I breathed a sigh of relief. With fifteen people and their luggage crammed into it, a minivan was bouncing its way toward Puno. I started waving at the van as it approached the stream. The driver crossed the stream, slowed down, stuck his head out of the window, and said something in *Español*. I pulled out my dictionary, but I couldn't see a word. All I could say after they stopped was, "*Por favor, ayudáis.*" Help was one of the first words I had read when I was in the hostel. The three men sitting on the front seat got out of the van, helped me pick up my bike, and started bombarding me with all kinds of questions. I couldn't even tell whether they were speaking *Español*. After they realized that I hadn't understood a word, they started the whole process again. When I said that I was trying to get to Moquegua, I could see the "Another stupid gringo" look on their faces. They told me that I could either go back to Puno, which would take another three hours, or ride for another half hour and stay in the small town there. It would have been safer to go back to Puno with them. But my whole plan was pretty ambitious. I wanted to go to the southern tip and come back. There was no point in turning back. I decided to keep going for another half hour and spend the night in the small town.

I reached the town a touch after eight o'clock. It was a village of less than fifty people, with a dirt road and ten huts on each side of the road. I saw a couple walking along the road and asked them whether there was a hostel in the village. They said there was nothing like that in the town. They pointed toward the only concrete structure in the village. I could see a small light glowing in its front porch area. The couple asked me to go there.

The people in the house came out before I reached the front porch. I guess they couldn't hide their curiosity. I used all my knowledge of *Español* to tell them that I was from India, I wanted to go to Moquegua, and that I was looking for a place to stay for one night. They huddled up and started discussing things in *Español*. After a few minutes, one of the guys noticed the anxiety on my face. It looked like he was the only guy who knew a few English words. "*No problema, no worry,*" he said in his broken English. After some more discussion with the other people in the house, he led me to the adjacent building.

He helped me park the bike in the corridor and showed me the room that they had allotted to me. It looked like a hospital room. There was a bed, an oxygen cylinder, an examination table, and a couple of charts about neonatal health and dental care. The couple that I had met on the street brought a couple of blankets for me. The man who knew a few English words abandoned English and started using sign language. He told me that there was no electricity in the town after nine o'clock. He also told me that it got really cold in the night. Of course, it would! This was four thousand meters from sea level. He pointed to a small, toaster-sized heater, told me to shut the door and the windows, and let the heater run until nine o'clock. *All right, sir! As you wish!*

I asked him whether I could get food anywhere in town. There was no restaurant in the town. But they arranged for a piece of bread and a cup of hot tea for me. That, my Gatorade, power bars, and water was my first dinner out of Cuzco—a dinner to remember!

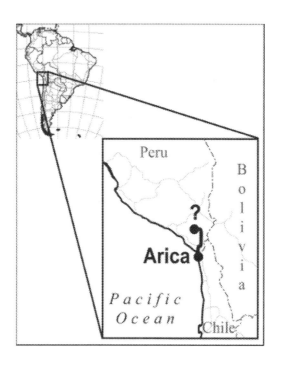

TWO:
From Heaven To Hell,
And Back To Earth

I woke up the next day and walked around the building. I wanted to know where the heck I was and who those people were. It looked like it was a primary healthcare center. They took me to the kitchen behind the building and gave me a cup of milk with some gooey stuff at the bottom. I sat down with the guy who knew a few English words and opened up my English-Spanish phrase book. As I was flipping through the phrase book to find the section on conversations, the guy suddenly felt the need to add some more words to my vocabulary.

He started pointing to the meat hanging by the roof. *Pollo. Carne. Pescado.* Stuff on the shelf. *Pan. Sal. Azúcar.* Damn, I had to learn how to say "Slow down, please."

His kid came running from somewhere and hid behind his chair. The man was a dentist from Tacna. He told me that he visited the small town every weekend. He was thirty-two and his kid was nine. I turned my attention to the kid. He said he loved *fútbol.* He was just waiting for school to reopen after the summer break so that he could start playing with his buddies again—or something like that! Hmmm … we were done with the basics. What would I ask now? It was time for me to get used to those weird and abrupt ends to the conversations.

"*Dolora da cabeza,*" I read out of the book. I asked the lady working at the healthcare center whether they had Aspirin. Riding in the freezing cold the night before had given me a terrible headache. She said they only had paracetamol and ibuprofen. I chose paracetamol. I turned my cell phone on and checked the time—almost eleven. It was time to leave. I took a couple of pictures of them and started packing my bag.

They never asked for money. They were not going to. Dentists who go from big cities like Tacna to villages of less than fifty people to serve them don't care about money. I paid them twice what I had paid to stay in Cuzco and hit the road.

The dentist had told me that I would be riding on dirt roads for at least three hours. But he didn't tell me anything about the terrain. For the first couple of hours, I was riding on dirt roads through streams and grasslands. And then, the whole landscape suddenly changed into a desert. I had at least come across a couple of shepherds with their llamas before I hit the desert. But there was literally *nothing* in the desert— no bushes, no streams, no rocks, no llamas. No trace of life. Range after range of sand. And some snow-clad peaks in the distance enjoying the view of the desert. After riding for more than half an hour in the desert, I saw a truck coming from the other side. It was the first vehicle of the day!

I pulled over and started waving at the truck. I asked the driver whether I was still on the right track. He told me that I would hit a fork in another half hour. There was a small hut at the fork. The guy in the hut was going to give me directions to Moquegua. Take that for directions! But my sense of relief?—priceless! I was on the right track, at least ...

Another half an hour and there it was: a fork, a hut, and three people sitting outside looking at the *loco* riding the bike. The two women went inside as I approached the hut. The man, with his hands on his hips, kept staring at me. I approached him and asked for directions. He told me that I was at the bottom of the hill and the paved road was at the top of the hill. He gave me two options: The first was to ride for three kilometers and go around the hill where the dirt road met the paved road. The other option was to ride for a kilometer straight up, get to the top of the hill, and take the paved road from there. I was still in the middle of a desert. The road straight up was full of sand. I asked him whether a 400-cc bike would go straight up. "*No hay problema*," he said confidently.

I took the risk, and paid for it. I had gone three quarters of the way up when the motorcycle gave in. I had already shifted to first gear, but I was riding over layers and layers of sand. The tires just couldn't find the solid ground under the sand. My bike, my backpack, and I were all left sitting in the sand, somewhere in the Andes. I started thinking about walking down the hill and calling the man up to help me out. Oops! The petrol was leaking from the air inlet tube of the motorcycle. I was in the middle of a desert with only one hut in sight and no other sign of life. I stuck my finger in the tube and started thinking about my next move. Was there anything around the motorcycle to stop the leak? After searching for fifteen minutes, I gave up and started thinking about ways to get some help. I looked up. I could see the edge of the paved road. But the road was deserted. My only hope was the man down in the hut. I started waving my other hand and screaming as loudly as I could. Five minutes passed, then ten minutes. Nothing. My voice was not reaching the hut. After another ten minutes, I saw the man walk out of the hut. I started waving and screaming again. Finally, he noticed me. *Phew!*

The hill was so steep that it took him twenty to thirty minutes to come up. How would I tell him that there was a petrol leak and that I wanted to plug it? I took my finger off the tube and let it leak for a few seconds. He searched around and got me a small stick to plug into the tube. We picked up the motorcycle and tried to start it. Nothing! It was a nasty mixture of a flooded engine, freezing cold, and low oxygen. He pointed to the hut and asked me to follow him.

By the time we got back to his hut, I was ready to collapse. Pushing the bike through the sand had worn me down. Our attempts to push the bike downhill and force it into second gear were not working. The battery looked okay, but we just couldn't get it to start. So he applied the choke and started playing around with the motorcycle. I quickly resigned to the bystander role. After a good half hour of us kicking and screaming, the bike finally roared back up. I paid the man whatever I could. But there are times when money just doesn't do it. I had already had two such moments in two days. I wish I could have expressed my gratitude, at least. But even things like, "I can't tell you how much this means to me" were out of my reach. A bunch of "*Muchas gracias*" was all I could find in my verbal desert.

I took the safer route and got to the paved road. As I went up the hill, I looked at the fuel gauge. Between the petrol leak, the engine flooding, and my starting it again, I had lost a lot of petrol. And there was no petrol pump before Moquegua. I turned off the engine as I was going downhill. After thirty to forty kilometers of riding downhill, I finally felt confident enough to start my engine. Moquegua was possible now. My circus finally ended in Moquegua around seven in the evening.

By nine o'clock I was in Tacna. A greasy chicken sandwich and I was ready to hit the sack.

My original plan had been to start from Cuzco, go down the western coast of the continent all the way to the southern tip, come back up along the eastern coast to Buenos Aires, head back to Santiago, and trace my way back to Cuzco. Alas! After my first three eventful days in Peru, I realized that my plan had been too ambitious. It was not possible to do five to six hundred kilometers a day for forty days. I decided to take it one day at a time.

The next day, I got to the Peru-Chile border and spent an hour completing all the border-crossing formalities. A statue of Jesus with his outstretched arms greeted me at the Peru-Chile *Friendship Line*. Apparently, Chile imposed the *Friendship Line* on Peru almost a century ago when they won a huge chunk of the desert in a war. Standing in the middle of the desert, it was hard to believe that anyone would fight for that piece of land. But, as Aristotle had once said, "The only people who've seen the end of war are dead people." I thought about sticking a note under the statue of Jesus which said: "Shut up, a*******. I'm the one who died for all your sins."

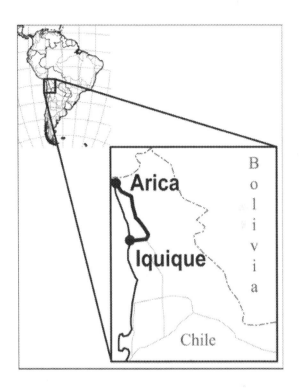

THREE:
The Perfect Storm

I am not sure whether the Peruvians like the Chileans. But it looks as if the Chileans don't really trust the Peruvians. I guess Peruvians are still considered second-class citizens in Chile. You could see it at the border crossing. All the Peruvians were patiently waiting outside, forming long lines in the sweltering heat. The Chilean authorities were herding the cattle when I stepped into the air-conditioned immigration office. After another Herculean effort of speaking *Español*, I reached Arica in the afternoon. Iquique, the next big city, was only about three hundred kilometers away. It didn't sound like a lot, but I didn't want to take the risk. I had learned my lesson.

Arica was my first stop in Chile. Chile was a country I had known nothing about just a few years ago, except for its location on the map. If it hadn't been for my Chilean advisor and lab-mate, I probably wouldn't have learned any more about Chile. This much I knew—Uganda: Idi Amin; Libya: Gaddafi; Zimbabwe: Mugabe; Vietnam: Ho Chi Minh; and Chile: Pinochet.

It was my first day in Chile. I hadn't really seen much, just a few kilometers of desert and a border town. But, in those fifty kilometers, I had gone from chaotic cities, dusty streets, and Native American features to a town with a clean plaza and a central street lined with fancy stores, upscale bars, nice restaurants, and distinctively European features. I checked in to a small hostel and dumped my backpack. As I started looking for a place to park my bike overnight, I finally learned that a parking lot is called an *estacionamiento*. Wow! It sounded like some badass palace.

Spanish is an interesting language. A lot of the commonly used words—like we: *nosotros*; you all: *vosotros*; work: *trabajar*; any: *cualquier*—are unusually long. And the changing verb forms make your life all the more miserable. The biggest challenge as a student of Spanish, though, was understanding where one word ended and the other one started. The whole sentence sounded like one word. Even after asking people to slow down, I was finding it incredibly difficult to parse the sentences. The confused look on my face would usually force them to rephrase their questions. And when that failed, they would just give up and end the conversation.

Victor, or *Bictor* in *Español*, gave me the directions to the nearest parking lot and a few good restaurants in the neighborhood. He was from the southern part of Chile and he had moved to Arica to manage the hostel so that he could earn and learn. He was pursuing a degree in tourism.

After an awkward pause, it was my turn to answer his questions. Judging by his barrage of questions, it seemed he was interested in knowing a lot about me. Maybe I was the first Indian person he had met. Again, my *Español* failed me. I just couldn't understand the questions he was asking me. Nonetheless, it was a great feeling. I was learning to ask some basic questions about parking and food in *Español*. Yes, the conversations were still ending abruptly, but it was a good start!

I stepped out to call my former Chilean colleague and tell her that I had finally reached her country. I was some two thousand kilometers away from her town, but I was on my way. It had been a while, more than a year, since I had talked to her. I had never thought that I would ever meet her or, for that matter, talk to her after she had moved back to Chile. But it feels nice to get a chance to reconnect with someone who used to be a part of your everyday life. My life had changed a lot. And I wanted to know about her life back in Chile. We had a lot of things to talk about. I dialed her phone and went straight to voice-mail. Bummer! It was fun to hear the voice-mail notification, though. I knew what it meant, but not because I understood the words. Oh well, she had told me about her summer vacation plans. She must still be on vacation.

Next stop was Iquique. Three hundred kilometers of nothing separated Iquique from Arica. I was about to cross the Atacama Desert, the driest desert on earth. The guy at the rental agency had told me that the motorcycle would go for about three hundred kilometers with a full tank. I was not going to leave without a full tank. No more stupid risks.

I stopped at the Copec gas station on the outskirts of Arica and asked the elderly gentleman whether there was any other gas station between Arica and Iquique. An enthusiastic young guy jumped into our conversation and told me that there were none before Iquique. When I told him that my *motocicleta* could go *trecientos kilometros* with a full tank, he started telling me that I should carry some extra fuel with me. While

I understood that he was trying to help me out, none of his words made sense to me. They were not in the list of *Español* words that I had learned to this point. *"Por favor, escribes,"* I said. He gave me a piece of paper with *Bidon para combustible* written on it. With sign language, he told me to go back to the city and buy one of those.

After an hour of walking around in the sweltering heat with the protective jacket and pants on, I finally found a five-liter container. As I was walking back to my bike, I stopped at one of the stores and asked for a glass of water. The store owner looked at me and asked me whether I was Pakistani. It was interesting that the owner of a small hardware store in a small border town like Arica had learned to associate brown skin and black hair with Pakistan. Why Pakistan?

When I said *"Soy de la India,"* his next question was, *"Ah, Hindu?"* In South America, being from India automatically makes you a Hindu. I wished I could tell him that we have more Muslims in India than they have in Pakistan. Another half hour of going through my phrase book! I drank the water, nodded at him, and moved on.

I traced my way back to the gas station, filled up the *bidon para combustible*, and left Arica. The ancient stone pillars built by the Native Americans were just outside of Arica—carefully crafted pillars of stone in the middle of nowhere. I looked around for some information about them, but there was none. It reminded me of some of the tourist sites in India, which were rich in history but crying out for help. Oh well, how many things am I going to worry about? Stop, click, and move on.

I had barely done a hundred kilometers when I noticed the plumes of dust filling up the sky. A couple of truck drivers emerging from the sand clouds waved their hands at me. I guess they were asking me to slow down. But I wasn't sure why. I had no idea that I was approaching the first desert storm of my life.

The winds started picking up and sand was in the air.

It felt like it was raining sand. As I entered the storm, my speed went down from eighty or ninety kilometers per hour to twenty. The winds started pushing me to the other side of the road. Visibility was down to ten or fifteen feet. An occasional sixteen wheeler was popping out of the sandy fog. So entering the other lane wasn't an option.

I started driving into the wind to keep the motorcycle from tipping over or drifting into the other lane. Fifteen minutes. Twenty minutes. It was getting worse. The winds were getting stronger. Sand had started creeping into my helmet, and the winds were trying to pull my head away from my body. It was a struggle to keep my head on my shoulders. I looked up for a moment, hoping to see some signs of the storm dying down. But there were none. It felt like that time between sundown and complete darkness. I had never imagined that a combination of wind and sand could change a bright sunny day into the twilight sky. I thought about pulling over for a while. But, with another two hundred kilometers ahead of me, I kept going. After a good half hour of riding through the desert storm, I felt the winds finally start to subside. Another ten minutes and everything was back to normal. After sticking my head out in the ninety- to one-hundred-kilometer-per-hour winds, with my helmet on, my neck was giving in. I pulled over, took my helmet off, and made sure that everything was all right. My neck was fine, but I had started having second thoughts about the whole trip.

In the next two hundred kilometers, there was exactly one police checkpoint, one oasis, with a population of less than hundred, and one restaurant, in the middle of nowhere. As I approached the police checkpoint, the police on duty stopped me and started asking me questions. All I could say was "*Lo siento, hablo mui poco Español.*" He gave up and let me go. After another ten minutes or so, I had that "aha" moment. I realized that he was asking "*De dónde eres?*" It was the Chilean accent. Omitting all the s's. The ups and downs in the tone. *The Lonely*

Planet had warned me about it. But I hadn't noticed it at the Peru-Chile border. Maybe it was because the immigration officers had learned to tone down their accent. So it was my first encounter with a real *Chileno*. No wonder the policeman let me go. If I can't understand "Where are you from?" it's tough to move to the next question.

Another desert storm welcomed me as I approached Iquique. This one was shorter, though. I knew the drill and crossed it in fifteen to twenty minutes. Then came the final descent to Iquique. The breathtaking view of the city from the top of the mountain made the whole ordeal worth it. It reminded me of the day I hiked the Grand Canyon, taking the final steps out of the canyon. Your body is dead, but your mind is anything but dead. You feel a sense of winning against nature, however inconsequential or stupid it is.

It was an incredibly beautiful city. A booming beach resort jetted into the ocean on one side and cut into the enormous sand dunes on the other. The bright yellow dunes glowing in the desert sun created an amazing contrast against the light blue Pacific Ocean and the colorful city down below. The *Hostal Internacional* was right on the beach. A tattooed electrician from San Francisco, a Canadian couple who had just finished college, two girls from *Alemania* who spoke four languages each and were studying *Español* in Argentina—it was my kinda place. As I entered the main lobby, I heard people speak English. It felt good to meet people who were speaking a language that I knew!

A long shower, a quick nap, and I was ready for the sunset. My first sunset with my own camera! I was in a typical beach resort: the clean beaches, the boulevard going along the beach, Toyotas and Hondas crowding the streets, Chilean police on well-bred horses patrolling the beaches; I took my shoes off and buried my feet in the sand. I enjoyed the evening breeze for a while and started taking pictures. It was a strange moment— no family, no friends, no books—just me and my camera. Two strangers brought together by a lonely adventure. I clicked away a few times and hung my camera around my wrist. I regarded the distant dunes. The receding waves. The bubbly water. And observed a moment of silence for the setting sun.

This was not the first time I had traveled. I had a lot of traveling experience under my belt. When I was a child growing up in India, my dad's passion for long road trips had helped me cover almost three-fourths of the country. At the height of the Indian summer, my parents, my older brother, my younger sister, and I would all be crammed up in a small Maruti 800 and driving all over the country. After moving back to the United States for graduate studies, I had covered about forty of the fifty states and almost all of the major cities of the States. I had enjoyed the tranquility of Okinawa, had lost myself in the crowds of Tokyo, and had tasted the laid-back lifestyle of a few Caribbean islands. I'd stood out, or stood short, in the robotic culture of Germany, saluted the queen in London, and immersed myself in the romantic beauty of the Lake District in England.

Compared to an average American or Indian, that was a lot of traveling. But I had always traveled with my friends or family. I had always had someone to share my joys and sorrows with, someone to share my likes and dislikes with, someone to agree and disagree with. This was different. It was just me.

As a kid growing up in India, I had never even thought about traveling by myself. Forget about traveling, I had never even thought about going to a movie by myself! Why would anyone want to travel by himself? Your friends, your family, your colleagues—they all define you. Why would you ever feel the need to find yourself? Or define yourself?

At age twenty-eight, there I was, on a crowded beach in some obscure little Chilean town. For the first time in my life, I was with myself. I was away from everything: family's or friends' expectations, boss's expectations, my own expectations, my dreams, my ambitions, my drive, my wishes, Indian society, American society, the girls that I loved, the girls that loved me. I was a nobody. Nobody knew where I was. And there was no way of finding out. Yes, there were people around me, but they were on the other side of the language barrier. The camera was stealing my sights, but my inner sounds were still safe. They were still mine.

I started reflecting back on my own journey, through South America and through life. The waves kept forming, seemingly out of nowhere. They brought joys and sorrows ashore. The receding one would form a new one. I thought about my three days on the road: the kind and helpful Peruvians and Chileans, the stunning landscapes, the nervous excitement before I had started the trip. I reflected on the excitement of first love! Hmmm, grad school! I thought of the thrill of scientific discovery, the dark days of desperation and failure, the highs of finding love, the lows of losing love, my parents' unconditional love, my childhood, winning my first scholarship, winning my second scholarship, failing to get into the college of my choice, leaving the Indian society and embracing American society, making new friends, clinging on to old friends, my old friends, my true friends, the nasty hazing scandal in college, the irreverent teens, the rebel in college, the missed chances, the girls who loved me, walking the tightrope of respecting their feelings …

My mind was enjoying the sounds of the crashing waves. But my stomach started complaining. I walked over to the nearby grocery store and started staring at the aisles full of all sorts of jars and cans. The pictures on them made sense, but the words didn't. Ramen noodles! When in doubt, pick noodles! Two packets of noodles, a big bottle of orange juice, and I was ready to mingle with the international crowd.

Backpackers seem to have a standard unwritten protocol of introductions. After exchanging pleasantries, everyone indulges in good-old America-bashing. Pour a drink, bash America, pour one more, bash America, another drink, bash America some more. By the end of this first phase, everyone has had a few drinks, and the conversation moves on to their goals in life, or the lack thereof. In my case, it took them a while to convince themselves that even though I'm an Indian neuroscientist with little knowledge of *Español* traveling through South America on a motorcycle on my own, I am not an alien. The professional stories are followed up by personal stories. And then, everyone religiously gets back to America-bashing.

It was a fun night. I was just happy to meet English-speaking people. Before leaving the next day, I rode around the old part of the town. It used to be a busy port during the nitrate boom in northern Chile. The city had a huge docking yard, an impressive plaza, and a long yellow government building that made up the old center of the city. As I found out later, yellow was the color of choice in the desert. After the collapse of the nitrate boom, the city had transformed itself into a beach resort—an impressive transformation!

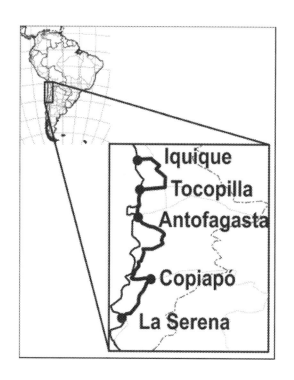

FOUR:
Chain-ed Melody

It was well past noon before I left Iquique. Antofagasta was well over four hundred kilometers away. The guy managing the hostel told me that I could take the route that goes along the coast to Tocopilla, which was halfway between Iquique and Antofagasta. But no one could tell me how to get to that road. I had to take the boring desert road. After a rather un-eventful four-hour journey through the empty desert, I was in Tocopilla, a small town with a small port and a small plaza. I found a cheap hostel owned by a Croatian family. Seeing no standard restaurants serving Italian or Mexican or American food, I went to the small eatery next door. The eatery had no menu, and the waitress started telling me about the food they had. This was another nightmare scenario for me! Her train was going full speed and I was just trying to catch on to something, anything. I heard her say something like *completo* and I jumped on it. I also ordered it *doble,* thinking that it would be a nice, greasy, loaded sandwich. All I got was two hot dogs topped with tomatoes and guacamole. Guacamole? An attempt to make the hot dogs look nutritious? Oh well, they were amazing, but not what I was expecting after a long day of riding.

Tocopilla was a dusty little town that denied the mountains to the east the pleasure of washing their feet in the Pacific. A chemical plant and a small port supported a community that looked like a pale shadow of its nitrate-boom days. A firehouse painted with a generous dose of bright colors stood out in the busy central bazaar. I took a few pictures, packed my bags, and was ready to head south. With only two roads leaving the city, it was hard to miss the one going south along the coast. The beautiful mountains, the ocean, and the winding road were all waiting for me—the *Ruta 1* of South America! It was an amazing ride, a paved road with a host of nitrate-era remnants—deserted towns and monuments along the road, cute little shades covering benches with nobody to sit on them, an abandoned seaside mansion with all sorts of graffiti on its walls. All were made beautiful by the ocean to the west.

The road was lined with graves, which were decorated with amazing detail. Why were these graves in the middle of nowhere? Were they there because the people had died there? Or did their loved ones want them to enjoy the beautiful sunsets every day of their afterlives? Where did the freshly burnt candles come from, and the beautiful flowers?

What if my life ends here? Would they know that Hindus don't bury their dead? Why am I thinking about death? … Why do we run away from death? What if there was no death? If I knew I was immortal, would I ever have booked that flight to Cuzco? Or would I just have kept talking about my desire to travel through South America on a motorcycle, just like a million other people do? If we were all immortal, would anyone ever travel anywhere? In a world of immortals, would anyone care about exploring the world or exploring other cultures? So should we start celebrating death for all the beautiful things that it makes us do while we are alive? A crash-course on immortality! Oh well, humming "Love is All You Need" was a lot easier! Long live the Beatles!

I was in Antofagasta before I could go through my list of all the Beatles, Pink Floyd, and Kishore Kumar songs. It was nice to experience the thing called city life again. I opened up my New Testament, *The Lonely Planet*. It said that Antofagasta was one of the biggest ports in Chile, a rough-and-tumble city with a mish-mash of old architecture, run-down neighborhoods, glitzy malls selling everything under the sun, brightly colored new buildings, all thrown into a huge melting pot. It was a place where you could find a bit of everything but it still felt empty. It was an imposing city without a soul, a city that was expanding without a purpose—kinda like life, right?

I spent the night in a run-down hostel and hopped on my bike in the morning. Next stop was Copiapó! The ride from Antofagasta to Copiapó was pretty monotonous. I was just happy to ride on roads with some people on them. Another night in another hostel, another long journey, and I was in La Serena, one of the oldest and most beautiful cities in Chile. A long, straight road, lined with trees, took me from the quiet beach to the loud and busy city center. It was the first time in my journey that I had to ask at four different hostels before finding a vacant room. It was good to know that there were so many tourists in the city.

By the time I reached La Serena, I had done a good two to three thousand kilometers. It was time for an oil change. I stopped at the first motorcycle repair shop and started in my broken *Español*. The manager quoted me ten U.S. dollars for oil and filter change. I started asking him how long it would take and whether they accepted credit cards. He realized that I was not good at *Español* and started searching for reasons to jack up the cost. He asked me whether I was carrying oil with me. He added another twenty dollars when I said no. Welcome to exploitation. He finally gave me a quote of forty dollars, and I agreed. He told me that one of the mechanics in his shop was good at English and suggested that I talk to him.

"How are you doing?" asked Juan.

"I'm fine, how are you?" I followed up. I complimented him on his English and asked him whether he had taken English courses in school. He told me that he had picked it up by listening to a lot of rock music. Impressive!

As he was working on my bike, I asked him a bunch of questions about Paso de Agua Negra—the pass of black water—a road that goes from La Serena to Argentina through the Andes. I had heard a lot of good things about it, but I wasn't sure about the road conditions. With all the pictures on the Internet showing a dirt road, I was not too keen on crossing the border through the Paso. But a part of me was still hopeful. Maybe they'd paved the road now! After all, it was the most developed developing country in South America. And tourism is one of biggest industries in Chile.

"The road is good, good," another guy jumped in. He started telling me in Spanglish that it was about forty-five hundred meters above sea level. He claimed that he had done it a few months ago. With the bike that I was riding, he thought it would be a cakewalk. I asked him repeatedly whether he was sure about the road conditions. Every time he told me that the road was good, I could feel the hopeful part of me growing. It was almost as if I were itching for my next small town, health-care center, and bread-and-tea adventure. They say success is addictive. I think it is risk taking that's more addictive. The next time I get into the whole small-town health-care center situation, I won't even feel like I've taken any risk. Been there, done that. I'll look for something more risky, more adventurous.

The mechanics were enjoying their first encounter with a Hindu. After a while, Juan told me that if I was planning to climb up forty-five hundred meters on that motorcycle, I needed to tighten the chain. He told me not to talk to the manager and said that I should go to their other workshop and get it done for free. When I asked him where the other workshop was, he told me that it was on the outskirts of the city. He said he was planning to get there by five in the evening and he wouldn't mind working on my bike after that.

I was in a foreign country, with a guy I had met ten minutes ago. I was on the outskirts of a big, touristy city. A bunch of motorcycle mechanics knew that I was a foreigner with minimal skills in *Español*. I had every reason to decline the offer. But, for some reason, I've always found believing strangers easier than believing people I know. My philosophy of people generally being nice forced me to take the bait. Besides, getting it done in the same workshop was not an option. I didn't want to be exploited again. If I followed his instructions, there was at least a chance of saving some money.

So, there I was, behind a lonely gas station on the outskirts of La Serena. A few sticks supported a huge sheet of plastic that was guarding a dismantled Beetle, two rusty motorcycles, and four men from the bright sun: Juan, his mechanic friend, and two policemen. While Juan was fixing the chain, one of the policemen noticed that the motorcycle had a Peruvian license plate and started asking me questions about it. I told him about my trip, but I didn't have the papers to prove that I had a valid visa and that I had rented the motorcycle in Peru. I had left all my documents back in the hostel. I could see him giving me a long stare from under his sunglasses. He let me go with a warning when he realized that I was staring right back at him.

I tried to pay Juan for his services, but he kept declining. It was a Thursday evening. I asked him whether he was planning to go out later in the night. He told me that there was only one bar in town that played his kind of music, classic rock and heavy metal. I offered to buy him a drink, and he readily accepted the offer.

It was a good opportunity for me. I had been on the road for more than a week, and I hadn't been to any of the local bars. It was time for me to break out of my shell. In a way, my first week in South America had reminded me of my first week in the United States. Being in a new culture, with new people, new mannerisms, and new language, you are measuring every step you take. But, after my first week on the road, it was time to get rid of my apprehensions about being in a foreign country and not knowing the language. Anyway, Juan was going to be there. That was a huge relief.

"*Ron con cola, por favor,*" I said as I was clearing my throat.

The bartender didn't understand my *Español* and asked me, "*Inglés?*" I nodded, with a smile—a perk of being in a touristy town! I was looking around for Juan, but all I could see was a drunken face sitting right next to me. He was smiling at me as if I were some strange, harmless creature, like the alien in E.T.! Funny what a stiff language barrier can do to you.

After a few minutes of searching in vain, I asked the bartender whether he knew Juan, the motorcycle mechanic. It was like asking for "Amit, the engineer" in India, but it was my last hope. When the bartender said no, my only option was to initiate conversations with strangers in *Español*. Within a few minutes of embracing that option, I found out that the drunken face staring at me was the face of a pretty successful distributor of toys. The man occupying the other stool was a taxi driver shuttling between the old La Serena and the young Coquimbo. For some reason, he was under the impression that people living in the United States say "What's up, man?" every five minutes. He had been studying tourism management in college when he ran out of money and became a taxi driver.

He tried talking me into going to Coquimbo in his taxi. But the manager of the bar stepped in and forced his friend Diego into the mix. With a hefty build, long curly hair, and square face, Diego barely spoke English. He drove the businessman and the taxi driver away and grabbed the stool next to mine. Diego was in his early thirties and was working in some ammunition factory. He had spent a few years in Spain and was boasting about sleeping with a lot of women. After a good half hour, the manager came back to check on us. I was struggling through my conversation with Diego. Luckily, the manager was good at English. *Phew!*

The manager was an artist who had spent most of his life in Valparaiso. I moved my attention to him and found out that he and his friends were huge fans of Pink Floyd. *Nice!* A new round of drinks. A discussion on music. After a few more *ron con colas* and "Brain Damage," they started wrapping things up. It was closing time. As I stepped out of the bar, Diego followed me and started walking me back home. "*Solamente cinco minutos,*" I said with a dismissive gesture. My hostel was just a few blocks away. It was not going to take me more than five or ten minutes to get there. But Diego insisted on escorting me back home. On our way back, I asked him whether he knew the businessman and the taxi driver whom he had kicked out earlier. He told me that the businessman and the taxi driver could have easily robbed me. Wow! And why did the manager save me? Why was he helping me? I looked at him and saw him smiling back at me. "*Mi hermano,*" I said, as we reached the hostel, and I gave him a hug.

As I was untying my shoes, my thoughts started drifting back to the bar episode. Should I feel good about the fact that I could speak with the locals, feel good about the manager and Diego protecting me? Should I feel sad about the everyday struggles in the taxi driver's life? Why do I always feel bad about people who are denied their share of opportunities? What if everyone got to do whatever they wanted to do? Would they be happy? If everyone got what they wished for, would anyone ever want to be a taxi driver? And then who would drive the taxis?

"Me and you,
God only knows,
it's not what we would choose
to do."
Roger Waters! Heaven!

FIVE:
Stairway To Heaven

I had ten to fifteen hours' worth of riding planned for the next day. Paso de Agua Negra was calling me. I stuffed three or four spoonfuls of Gatorade into my mouth and washed it down with a few glasses of water. Five hours of sleep, and I was ready to tie my backpack onto the carrier of the motorcycle. I thought about leaving a bottle of rum at the gas station for Juan, but it was too early in the morning to buy anything.

I passed one motorcycle on my way to the Chile-Argentina border. *Nice!* I wasn't the only crazy guy trying to cross Paso de Agua Negra alone on a motorcycle. I was at the Chilean checkpoint within a couple of hours. The guard at the check-point told me that the actual *frontera* was unmanned and that there was nothing but the road for the next couple hundred kilometers. I had to cross the Andes to join human civilization again. Would there be accumulation along the way? Would I ride into a snowstorm? There was no Weather Channel there!

What I expected to be a hung-over ride from sea level to forty-five hundred meters and back down turned out to be one of the most amazing rides of my life. As I started climbing up the mountains, I realized that I was riding through the most colorful ranges that I had ever seen. The gods of volcanoes have chosen the canvas of the Andes to produce a stunning piece of modern art at Paso de Agua Negra. It's as mysterious as it is easy to appreciate. I was riding through an enormous collage of red, green, yellow, brown, and black mountains created by the volcanoes. With every stroke of new color, the volcanoes were trying to say that they are not as evil as people make them out to be. As I approached the summit of one of the mountains, it gave way to an enormous lake of black water. At the top of the Andes, looking at those colorful mountains and dirt roads, and staring into the deep gorges and the black water, I felt a certain dizziness. I was left speechless with the beauty of it all. I shared a quiet moment of reflection with the tranquil waters and resumed my uphill trek through the ranges of dark red mountains. As if all this were not enough, I noticed some snow-clad peaks at a distance with a glacier running down one of the peaks. For the first time in my journey, I wished I could just sit back and enjoy the scenery. I wished someone else was driving the motorcycle.

I finally reached civilization on the other side of the An-des after a grueling seven- or eight-hour ride through the dirt roads of the Andes. Argentina—the land of Perón and Diego Maradona! The immigration office was a two-room outpost in the middle of nowhere. The four officers had their ears glued to a small radio in one of the rooms. They were following some local game of *fútbol*. It took the Argentinean immigration officer five or ten minutes to unglue his ears and pick up his stamp. He started going through my passport as if it were some museum artifact. He started asking me about every single stamp on my passport. When I told him that my parents lived in India and that I visited them pretty often, he asked me why my birthplace was Chicago. When I tried telling him that my parents had been in the United States when I was born, he passed a ruling that I was a pretty complicated case.

He changed his line of questioning. He now wanted to know why I had visited *Japón*, or Japan. When I told him that I was a neuroscience student and that I had visited Japan to attend a workshop, he realized that understanding why my place of birth was Chicago was easier. Trying to understand my academic background was much more complicated. After a failed attempt at understanding what neuroscience was, he just stamped my passport and let me go. I found a three-dollar-per-night hostel and paid five dollars for a heavy Argentinean steak dinner. It was a perfect topping on a perfect day. I was a happy man.

*   *   *

Riding up and down the Andes in one day had worn me down. The next morning I took my own time to get up and get on my motorcycle again. In less than an hour, I was on the historic *Ruta Quarenta,* or Route 40, made famous by Che Guevara. I was hoping to see a lot of motorcycle drivers on Route 40, but I was thoroughly disappointed. Except for an occasional car or truck, the road was pretty much empty. An hour later, a city-wide *siesta* welcomed me to San Juan. It was the middle of the day, but the city was dead. The weather was nice, and I was not feeling tired. I just needed some Argentinean pesos to fill up my tank and move on, but the banks were all closed. I had two hours to kill. After a lazy lunch and a lazier stroll around the plaza, I was finally able to smell some Argentinean pesos.

Next stop was Córdoba. It was at least ten hours from San Juan. I checked the time. It was almost five in the evening. It was not possible. With Vallecito just an hour away, I decided to knock it off of my long ride to Córdoba.

The shrine at Vallecito turned out to be the Argentinean *Jai Mata Di*. The legend has it that the woman who died there started in San Juan and followed her warrior husband till Vallecito. She took her last breath on the hill while breastfeeding her child—or something like that. It was hard to tell how that translated into her being the good-luck charm for all the truckers and travelers—as if people care about logic when it comes to good-luck charms!

It was a strange shrine, though. The devotees had not left any open space on the pillars or the ceiling of the walkway. Everything that could be used to decorate trucks was hanging off the stairs, railings, and walls of the shrine. It was also the first place on earth where I had seen people dedicating their license plates to a deity. Heaven's DMV?

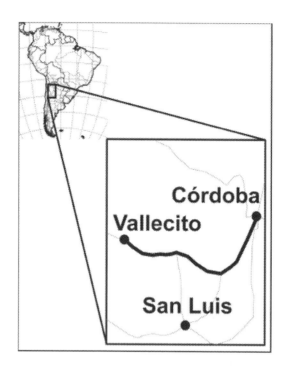

SIX:
A Boxful Of Life

It was going to be another long ride. Córdoba was at least ten hours away. I started early in the morning. As I was leaving Vallecito, I noticed a couple of hitchhikers at the intersection of the local road and the highway: a hippie and a hippie-ish guy. The small hippie in me made me pull over and ask them where they were headed. "Buenos Aires," they shouted in unison. As they were approaching me, I told them that I was going to Córdoba and that I wouldn't mind giving one of them a ride. The hippie jumped at the offer. He didn't have a helmet, but I asked him anyway. He said that he didn't care and tied his stuff, one small cardboard box, onto my backpack. I had no idea that I was about to start the most memorable leg of my journey.

Within half an hour, we were ready to enter the state of La Rioja. I didn't expect the police at the checkpoint to pull us over for the helmet law. But there they were, asking us to slow down. The cop asked us to step aside. After the initial ritual of examining all my papers, the policeman asked me why my friend was not wearing a helmet. I tried to pretend that I didn't understand the question, but I realized that I was in for some trouble. I tried the "*Hablo poco Español*" ploy, but that was exactly the kind of guy the cop was looking for. He sent me to the other cop, who was sitting at the checkpoint, and resumed his patrolling duties.

The cop at the checkpoint examined my papers and asked my friend for his identification card. He had none. "Amigo?" the policeman asked me, as he was jotting down my friend's name and address. I told him that I had picked the hippie up at San Juan. The cop started telling me that I had broken the law by allowing the hippie to ride with me without a helmet. When the policeman realized that the *Español* was getting too complicated for me, he flashed the rule book in my face. He pointed to the clause in the book that said that I owed them three hundred pesos in penalties. They said I'd have to go back to San Juan, pay the fine, and show them the receipt if I wanted to cross over into La Rioja. That was my first hint! There was room for negotiation. I had to be careful. I was in a foreign country. I didn't want to get caught bribing a police officer in a country where I barely spoke the native language. But there was definitely some room for negotiation.

I brought up my helpless face and tried to tell him that I did not know the law. "*Lo siento. Necessito llegar Córdoba este noches,*" I said. The cop acted as if he was not interested. I dug deeper and found another useful line. "*Yo se ahora. No más infracciones.*" The cop changed his line of questioning and started asking me about my parents. Another hint! After lecturing me for ten minutes about the dangers of riding without a helmet, he spelled out his first offer. He said I could either pay three hundred pesos in San Juan or pay one hundred and fifty pesos at the checkpoint. "*Estudio en Estados Unidos. Tengo poco dineros,*" I was trying my best not to laugh. He tried suggesting that I could also pay in dollars. After another five minutes, he finally asked me how many pesos I had. Yesssssss!

He flipped out when he heard me say that I had only twenty pesos. He started pretending he had had enough of me and pulled out his citation book. When I urged him again to accept the twenty pesos and let me go, he asked me to go back to San Juan, call my dad in India, ask him to wire some money, pay the fine, and then come back.

The more illogical he was getting, the closer I was getting to a settlement. He pulled out his pen but stopped just before he started writing a citation. Another lecture about road safety followed. And my apologetic face finally won the battle. He accepted the twenty pesos that I had offered and told me to drop my friend off at the next town. The sweet smell of victory!

As I was leaving the checkpoint, I couldn't help but wonder whether there was some universal code of corruption. Linguists debate whether language and grammar are coded into our genes. But I was interested to see that cops separated by an entire continent and having no cultural ties to each other had come up with the same procedure to condone traffic violations—for a small fee. The initial façade of incorruptibility, the unrealistic alternatives, outrage at the counter-offer, lectures about the importance of lawful behavior, and then the money exchanges hands. Language barrier? What language barrier?

We stopped for lunch in the next village. It was just a bunch of huts scattered in the middle of the endless plains of Argentina. I was pleasantly surprised to find out that one of the huts was a restaurant, a small *comedor*. I was wondering whether my friend was going to pay me back for the bribe.

More importantly, I wanted to tell him that I had no intention of paying bribes for him all the way to Córdoba. As we walked in, an old lady walked out and gave us a choice of beef or chicken. I chose beef. I was in Argentina! The counter was lined up with all kinds of bottles filled with soda. I chose the local version of Sprite. My amigo was not ordering anything. He said he was not hungry and offered me a peso to share the drink.

As we were waiting for food, I started my Herculean task of figuring out what his thoughts about going forward were. Bribing every policeman at every checkpoint was risky business. After five minutes of playing *Lost in Translation*, we resorted to sign language. He told me that the way to make it work was for him to get down a kilometer or two before the checkpoints, me to cross the checkpoint on my own, wait for him on the other side, and him to walk across the checkpoint and join me again. I didn't respond to that. It was a ten or twelve-hour ride and he wanted me to spend an extra hour at every checkpoint for him. We moved on to the standard "Where are you from?" and "What do you do?" while the lady was serving the steak. He was a struggling artist from Mendoza and made money by selling handmade bracelets and necklaces. I thought that he was just visiting Buenos Aires and coming back. *"Por que Buenos Aires?"* I asked. He told me that he was a nomad. He didn't have a home or a hometown. He was planning to spend a few months in Buenos Aires before coming back to Mendoza. Hmmm, sounded like a true hippie.

Apparently, his family was full of musicians. And he hadn't heard of neuroscience. He had one girlfriend in Mendoza and another in Buenos Aires, and all of them seemed to be enjoying their lives. They were not worried about their futures, not concerned about job security, and not jealous about the other woman. Everything was in harmony!

By the time we got to music, I had finished my salad and steak—the best I've ever had in my life. The lady had also served some bread, which I hadn't touched. A few minutes later, my amigo asked me whether I was going to eat the bread. When I said no, he jumped on it. He soaked it into the watery liquid on my plate and finished the two pieces of bread. I was taken aback by that. Why had he refused to share my steak when I offered it to him, then? Was he just trying to be modest? Was he really that poor? Did he only have one peso with him? Damn, I was being so selfish. I had to take him to Córdoba.

Crossing the other two borders was fun. I had a feeling of helping a struggling artist mixed with a sense of getting cheap thrills. We were stopping every half hour or forty-five minutes to stretch our butts out, and, of course, at the state borders. He would roll his own cigarettes, relish them till the last puff, and we would hit the road again. I tried starting a conversation about politics and Argentina's woman president. But he was clearly not interested in deadbeat issues like politics. Music and art were his topics. He told me about all the instruments that his family members played. All his friends were artists: painters, sculptors, craftsmen, *artistas*. No one was worried about the next meal; no one was worried about paying their bills, about retirement accounts, about wars or economic crises. It was as simple and uncomplicated as it could get!

We shared the sunset with our loves—he with his carefully rolled cigarette and I with my thoughts—as we were riding up a mountain. It was ten o'clock at night when we reached the top of the mountain. The temperature had dropped significantly, and we were still seventy to eighty kilometers from Córdoba. He didn't need my sunglasses anymore, but he definitely needed a jacket. And I needed a coffee to survive the last hour of riding. We pulled over into a rest area with a restaurant and a convenience store. I unpacked my backpack to pull out my jacket for him. He went straight to the convenience store and showed the owner some of his art. As I gave him my jacket, he handed over five or six of the necklaces in his box to the owner. The owner came back with a brown bag full of fresh, hot empanadas. He wore the jacket and offered me one of the empanadas in the bag. "Is that your dinner?" I asked him casually as I was finishing my empanada. He nodded sheepishly as he reached in for another empanada. It took me a few minutes to realize it, but he had just exchanged some of his art for food. It looked like he really didn't have any money. And I had just stolen a portion of his dinner. Should I return the leftover empanada? Or would that be disrespectful? I peeked into his box. All I could see was a change of clothes, some necklaces, and some bracelets. That was it! As they say, the earth was his bed and the sky his roof.

I quietly walked away, got a cup of coffee, and sat on the stairs. My left hand was holding my head, my right hand was pushing coffee into my body, and my eyes were staring blankly at the empty sky. How do you survive on a box?

The last hour/hour and a half was a drag. I could feel the effect of the coffee dying down as we approached the lights of Córdoba. After stumbling around and taking a couple of wrong turns, we finally arrived at the plaza that he wanted to go to. Another member of his brethren approached our bike as he was returning my jacket and unpacking. The other guy didn't seem to know my amigo. But it took them less than a minute to go from being strangers to being brothers. A few minutes later, the new brother turned his attention to me. He started bombarding me with questions. I guess he was asking me whether I was looking for a place to sleep. I am sure they would have put me up for a night. I thanked him for his offer and told him that I was planning to spend the night in a hostel. As I was stuffing my jacket back in the bag, my amigo reached out for a hug and kissed me on my cheek. My first Argentinean friend!

I checked my map and revved up the engine. I looked up and saw my amigo join a group of five or six hippies at the corner of the plaza. As I was riding away, I could see all of them bowing to me. It looked like my amigo had already told them about our journey together. They were probably trying to express their gratitude. And I was still feeling ashamed about accepting one of his empanadas. I waved at them and looked back as I was turning the corner. I saw my dreadlocked amigo with his hands clasped together over his head. Yes, we had just created an unwritten bond.

At the hostel, I washed my stinky socks and crashed onto the top of the bunk bed. As I closed my eyes, I started thinking about the artist. Why had that experience been so special to me? Poverty wasn't new to me. I had spent half of my life in India! The idea of poor people living within their means and not complaining about it wasn't new to me, either. I had spent half of my life in India! It took me back to my days as a starry-eyed teenager volunteering for the National Literacy Mission. I picked up the books, the slate, and the pencils that the school gave me and headed straight to the house of a cowherd. He used to live with his wife and two kids in a small hut. He was supporting his family by taking care of the cows and selling milk every day. At his age, he lacked the drive and energy to go out and educate himself. So there I was, walking into his hut twice a week, teaching him how to write, reviewing his homework, and adding new words to his vocabulary.

There was no escaping the smell of cow dung. The cows were right there, tied next to the hut. Calling the hut clean was a stretch. But the broad smile on his face after learning each new word was worth all the effort. There was only one dim bulb lighting his entire hut. But his glowing face made the whole hut look brighter. It was a beautiful feeling, a feeling of adding a new dimension to his life—teaching him how to hold a pencil, teaching his muscles to make all those tiny little squiggly lines called letters, empowering him to read and write—to go out there and learn things on his own, to understand how the world around him worked.

Then, just like that, we approached the last day of our little school. It was time to say good-bye. He read me a full story from Aesop's book and signed his name on a clean sheet of paper. We shared a hug, and I walked away.

It had been a great learning experience for me. I had learned how difficult it was to teach someone skills that had never entered my conscious thought process—putting myself in my student's shoes and working my way up; getting him excited about the next session; making sure that he didn't give up. But—that was it. His limited means, his simple life, his positive attitude, his family's hospitality—it was all there for me to see. But I was completely oblivious to all that. As a high-school kid, I was not even aware of the bigger picture. For me, the whole experience was a pleasant distraction. Building my own life was more important than understanding his life. As I grew up in a typical overeducated and protective Brahmin family, pursuit of good grades and degrees reigned supreme. Playing the role that the society had chosen for me was all I was supposed to do. Everything else took a backseat.

And now, there was this lonely road trip. Having spent twenty-eight years acquiring degrees, I had learned a lot about how machines and brains work. But how does *life* work? Taking a time-out from my robotic life was helping me understand that. It was my personal evolution. Like the random process of mutations leading to stronger, faster, and smarter species, my aimless wandering and bumping into strangers was helping me become a better human being.

Bumping into my amigo was one such random event. I don't know where he slept that night. It was definitely not as comfortable as the hostel bed that I got. And I don't know where he disappeared the night after. For some reason, I just wanted to see him again. I didn't have anything to say to him. But I still wanted to see him again, to see him selling his art and making good money—enough money to afford his next meal, so that he wouldn't have to wait for someone else's left-overs. I went to the same plaza the next day and noticed a few other artists who had set up shop on small pieces of cloth. But I couldn't find my amigo. I would not see him again.

*   *   *

What do we need for survival—a bagful of stuff for forty days—or a boxful of stuff for a lifetime? And why do we feel sad when we don't get what we want? Do we really need the things that we want? Where do we draw the line?

I will always wonder where my amigo is and how he is doing. He touched my life and taught me one of the biggest lessons. Will he ever wonder whether I finished my trip? Will he remember me? Or was I just another guy who helped him get from Vallecito to Córdoba? I am sure he would have found someone else if I hadn't offered him a ride. Maybe it wasn't so special for him. But *I* was not going to forget *him*.

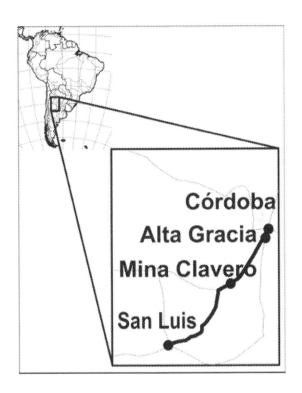

SEVEN:
Meeting Of Minds

The long ride, the sudden changes in weather, and the sharing of the small seat with my amigo had worn me down. It took me more than twelve hours to open my eyes again. I dragged myself out of the bed and dumped myself on the comfy couch in the lounge.

It was the third week of my vacation, and I was still seven hundred kilometers away from Buenos Aires. I was lazing around in the lounge, watching the news and looking at the maps. Seven hundred kilometers was a lot. I was contemplating turning around and heading back, when a tall, slender white guy with wavy brown hair walked in.

"*Quieres comer?*" he asked.

"*Hablo poco Español*," I replied, putting my dumb face on for the millionth time. I knew *comida*, but I hadn't made the *comer-comida* connection yet.

"*Desayuno?*" he rephrased his question. I had read that word in all the restaurant menus, and I knew it meant breakfast.

"*Sí*," I replied. I am not sure what made him ask me to join him for breakfast. And I don't know why I agreed to join him when my *Español* was so bad. Maybe it was because it sounded better than watching the CNN news by myself or because I was just trying to avoid thinking about turning around. Whatever it was, I started following the lanky Brazilian down the stairs. I had no idea that I was walking into one of the most intriguing friendships of my life!

We joined three more guys waiting for us downstairs: a Swiss, a Chilean, and a Uruguayan. It was an interesting mix: a Brazilian accountant working in Buenos Aires, a Swiss banker working for the Swiss Bank, a Chilean teacher working with children with special needs, and a Uruguayan student of anthropology. We were all in our carefree twenties—looking for chicks, looking for inspiration, looking to escape from the daily grind, looking for ourselves, or just floating around and bumping into people.

The bakery was just two blocks away. By the time we got to the bakery, Miguel, the Brazilian guy, had managed to get directions from a dozen girls. He looked like a typical early-twenties guy, trying to strike up a conversation with every other girl he was bumping into, hoping that one of the conversations would lead to something more. With my vast knowledge of *Español*, I had taken up the role of backseat-walking and asking the harmless "Where are you from?" questions occasionally. With our choice of attire, it was clear that we did not belong to Córdoba, so, when he asked for directions, some women just kept walking without even acknowledging my Brazilian friend's existence. Some stopped, answered the questions with mistrust boiling under their calm faces, and walked away. And then, there were some who indulged in long conversations, their veils of mistrust giving way to pleasant surprise and excitement at meeting five guys from five different countries. It was fun to observe the attitudes of all those women toward us. Millions of humans, over thousands of years, have developed hundreds of cultures and religions. Basic male and female instincts—they stay the same!

We were discussing our trip plans over breakfast, when Miguel and I realized that we were headed in the same direction. I asked him whether he wanted to join me on my *moto*. He gave me the are-you-kidding-me? look and moved on to the next topic. A few minutes later, he had a look of nervous excitement on his face. He started asking me questions about the motorcycle, the road conditions, and the price of a new helmet. He kept postponing his decision, partly because he had never ridden a motorcycle before. But he was definitely interested. "*Seguro?*" he kept asking me every few minutes. I told him that he had twenty-four hours to decide.

We started discussing plans for the day. The wannabe-hippie in all of us decided to avoid the touristy plazas and monuments in Córdoba and head to a lake and a waterfall nearby. We hopped onto the next bus to the lakeshore. While the rest of us were busy dozing off in our seats, Miguel was busy chatting up the locals on the bus. He managed to strike up conversations with a good twenty or twenty-five people in our one-hour journey. It was not just the chicks. Young and old, black and white, men and women—there was no discrimination. They were all smiling, frowning, fuming, complaining, and laughing with him. He would occasionally point to all of us and name our countries. That was our only contribution to their discussion. *Damn, I had to learn Español!*

We spent a few minutes at the lakeshore and started our hike up the stream to get to the waterfall. What was meant to be a short hike turned out to be a four-hour long ordeal. I didn't mind it—anything but motorcycle riding! As we were taking our final steps toward the waterfall and the lake, the heavens opened, and we all started scrambling for cover. After securing all our belongings, the motley crew with me started preparing for its smoking-pot-in-the-rain ritual. And then, the stories started flowing: the first time they had smoked pot, the last time they had smoked pot, the attempts to quit, the reasons not to quit. Then came the ritualistic bragging: the challenges of traveling with pot and the solutions. I was just standing there, trying to avoid second-hand pot smoking.

After four hours of hiking and pot smoking, we traced our way back to the hostel. On our way back, I looked around for my hippie amigo at the plaza. I was a bit disappointed when I didn't find him. But it was to be expected. It was time to get back to the hostel. After a long, hot shower and a couple of bowls of pasta, I was ready to hit the sack. I told Miguel that he had till nine in the morning to decide and buy a helmet. It was ten at night when I finally closed my eyes.

At one in the morning, I was forced to open my eyes again. The entire hostel was heading to a club. "I'm tired" or "I have to leave early tomorrow" were just lame excuses! Switzerland, Chile, Brazil, Uruguay, India, Canada, England, and Spain—the U.N. delegation was ready to dance!

As we were walking down the streets of Córdoba, the coffee shops, bars, and lounges were all packed. It's a city of a dozen or so universities and countless other colleges—always young. But it was summertime. I was hoping that the students in Córdoba would all be on vacation. No crowds, empty clubs—that would give me a chance to go back early and get enough rest for the long ride to San Luis the next day. But the long line outside our club dashed all my hopes of getting to sleep early. It was six in the morning when the sun finally started convincing the crowd to call it a day—or, a night. After a quick stop for some hot dogs, we finally got back in the hostel at seven in the morning. Now, that's what I call partying! I have heard a lot of economists talk about globalization and twenty-four-hour work cycles. Meanwhile, Latin American countries have perfected the art of twenty-four-hour *life* cycles!

I had two hours to go. I wasted an hour on the Internet and started packing my bag. I thought that after a full day of hiking, and a full night of partying, Miguel would not wake up before noon. But I was shocked when I walked out of the bathroom, and saw him in the waiting room. He was asking me to hurry up! He had packed his bags before going to bed. All he needed was a helmet.

Our first stop was Alta Gracia, Che Guevara's teenage hometown. It was only thirty kilometers from Córdoba, but it started pouring when we were on the outskirts of Córdoba. It was not the best time to find out that my jacket was not waterproof. By the time we got to Che's house, we were wet to the bone.

Miguel was already having second thoughts about the whole idea. He had started thinking about going back to Córdoba and catching a bus to San Luis. But somehow the museum, the motorcycle replica, maps of the roads Che had ridden on, and all the anecdotes of Che's travels inspired him to stick to the motorcycle plan. We waited for the rain to die down and hopped onto the motorcycle again. The initial excitement didn't last too long, though. Fatigue and exhaustion took over. After a tough four-hour ride through the treacherous mountains and bone-chilling winds, I was even ready to crash into the annoying truck in front of me to end the torture. Luckily, the resort town of Mina Clavero came to our rescue. After another steak dinner (at an artificially inflated price), we were both ready for a good twelve hours of sleep.

We spent the next day doing all the touristy things Mina Clavero had to offer. It was an interesting town: a rocky landscape with a river flowing through it. All kinds of waterfalls—tall and short, wide and narrow—created ponds of all shapes and sizes. People of all ages walked along the central boulevard. It was a typical tourist town for families.

Miguel was busy experiencing everything Mina Clavero had to offer, from jumping off the cliffs into the water to sliding along the rocky riverbed. While he was running around, I was busy admiring the beauty of the rich girls of Buenos Aires who were sunbathing on the rocks along the river. He wanted to spend another night and mingle with the rich crowd there. Unfortunately, I had neither the time nor the inclination to hang out with them. We finished the rest of the things on his list and left Mina Clavero in the evening. By the time we reached San Luis, he was tired of squeezing his butt onto half a motorcycle seat. He had gone through enough butt pain to realize that excitement alone was not enough to go cross-country on a motorcycle. But he also looked happy with the fact that he would finally be seeing the girl he had met at some concert in Buenos Aires.

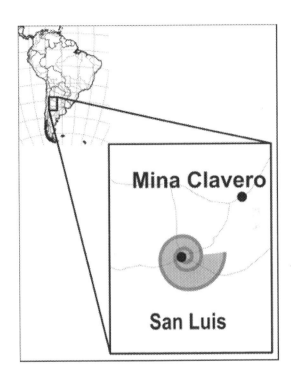

EIGHT:
Boy Meets A Girl, Family
Adopts A Kid

Rendezvous—it was Paula's favorite underground bar. Miguel and I took a quick nap and pulled out our bottle of rum. Our hostel had a small, well-kept backyard. It was a bright full-moon night, with clear skies and crisp air. For some strange reason, we started talking about stars and constellations. Miguel believed in astrology, and it looked like he knew his stars. He pointed to the scorpion in the sky and started telling me the story behind the constellation. It didn't take us too long to realize that it was getting lost in translation. We moved on to more mundane stuff like girls, love, and lust. He told me how he had met Paula at a Sting concert in Buenos Aires and started singing "Walking on the Moon." Like the alcohol in our bodies, our discussion about girls and love started taking all the familiar twists and turns. The language of missed chances, one-way streets, right person-wrong times, and wrong person-right times has no barriers. Pretty soon the bottle was empty, and it was time to hit the underground bar.

It was a dimly lit place with a small bar in the far corner. Tables and chairs were sprayed all over the floor. All those future Black Sabbath, Green Day, and Wailers members of Argentina had brought their own beers, cigarettes, weed, needles, and pills. We sat down with our humble *ron con colas* and resumed our never-ending language lessons. I learned a few more Spanish words, and Miguel learned a few more English words. For the hundredth time, he was telling me why he was so excited about meeting Paula. That's when she walked in with her boyfriend. She was just like Miguel had described her: a beautiful girl stepping into adulthood, with a face that still held on to its innocence. Miguel was happy to see her, but not as happy to see her boyfriend.

After the initial round of introductions, we started exchanging our stories. By that time, I had learned how to tell my story in *Español*. They went through the usual expressions of surprise and shock when they heard my story. After a few minutes, Miguel took Paula to the side to catch up with her. And Paula's boyfriend started asking me about my journey. I had no intention of talking about my journey or my life. I started asking him about his life. He told me that he was a jazz musician, a pianist. Now, that was much more interesting! Our discussion moved to Indian classical music. I was pleasantly surprised to find out that Paula's boyfriend and one of his friends, who had joined us, were huge fans of Ustad Zakir Hussain and Ustad Amjad Ali Khan. They started asking me all kinds of questions about Indian classical music. I started with the basics. But for some reason, Miguel was not interested in hanging out at the bar anymore. The fact that Paula had a boyfriend hastened our exit from there.

As we were walking back to the hostel, Miguel told me that Paula wanted to hang out with us the next day. He said she was in love with the jazz musician but still wanted to meet us. Apparently, her boyfriend was not going to be with her. He was still hopeful!

It was another lazy morning after a long ride to San Luis and a long night of drinking. We packed the three things that Paula had asked us to bring with us—swimming gear, sunscreen, and money—and started walking toward the bus stop. As we were waiting for Paula, Miguel told me that we were going to spend the day at her summer house, which was an hour away from San Luis. With sleep on my mind, I didn't ask too many questions. He was excited about the fact that her boyfriend was not going to be there, and I was just playing along.

Paula walked in and interrupted our conversation about her. We got onto the bus to whatever town it was. I raced to the last row, a fun place for people-watching. The driver hopped on a few minutes later. As he was closing the door, a middle-aged guy wearing the Argentinean blue stripes got on board. He started walking up and down the aisle and launched into some kind of speech in *Español*. It was hard for me to keep up with him, as he started talking about his family. I was trying to pick up as much as I could. It sounded like he was talking about the glory days and Argentinean pride, inserting *Jesus Maria* in his speech after every dozen or so words. He looked a bit too well-dressed and well-trimmed to be a beggar. He rambled on for another ten minutes, urging us to help him raise his kids. He went up and down the aisle, collected all the money he could, and got down at the next stop. It was a strange contrast to the Argentina around me: a once-rich country with good infrastructure, nice hostels, fancy restaurants, people with summer homes, teen punk-rockers searching for themselves, and beautiful women spending a lot of money on their appearance. But, away from the media glare, the glitzy TV shows, and the rich lifestyles of the soap operas, it looked like the economic meltdown of the late '90s was still hurting the small towns. The beggar in the bus, artists at the plazas, kids working in the parking lots, people searching through garbage cans looking for something—anything—valuable. It looked like they still had a lot of catching up to do.

The rest of the journey was uneventful, yet interesting. Cell phones and iPods were shielding half of the Argentinean ears from the outside world. Meanwhile, the Argentinean eyes were busy converting their passing glances into long, hard stares. It was probably the first time a lot of those San Luis*ians* had seen an Indian man. Americans have invented fake smiles to get out of the awkward long-stare situations. Unfortunately, the rest of the world hasn't really felt the need to invent anything like that.

Those stares on the bus reminded me of my stops at all the gas stations. It was fun to see the reactions of the gas station attendants: from *Just another guy*, to *He looks like me, but not quite*, to *Damn, where is this guy from?* to finally asking, "Where are you from?" and ending with a polite, "You are crazy." The gas station attendants, at least, asked a few questions. But the people on the bus were not interested in that. Those cell phones and iPods of all the staring eyes had robbed me of that escape route. All I could do was try to ignore their stares.

Paula's summer home was a well-kept bungalow surrounded by all kinds of trees and vines. She introduced us to her grandmother and her cousin before we started heading toward the river. It was a one-hour walk on a road lined with huge ranch houses, the summer escapes of rich Argentina. The long road ended in huge pillars of rocks. Flowing through those rocks of all shapes and sizes, the river reminded me of the landscape of Mina Clavero. The water was cold, and the river had a strong current due to the unusually heavy downpour of the weeks past. So swimming was not an option. We searched for a quiet bend and a flat rock for sunbathing and started discussing the religion, culture, and the history of Argentina. We discussed Paula's background, Miguel's background, and my background. As their interest in Hinduism waned, Miguel started asking Paula questions about her boyfriend. I picked up my stuff and moved to another flat rock, as he was trying to get cozy with her.

Miguel was in his early twenties, with the rest of his twenties of playing around ahead of him. From what he had told me, it seemed like he had some special feelings for Paula. But, having dated half a dozen girls and considering the possibility of more in the future, he was not sure whether he was ready to tell her about his feelings. And, having found her first love in the jazz musician, Paula was not sure whether holding someone else's hand, kissing someone else, or having feelings for someone else were appropriate. While they were busy growing up, I was lying in the sun, busy with my own rebirth after twenty-eight years. I had started out with sign language. Three weeks into my journey, I had expanded my vocabulary, learned how to parse sentences, and begun replacing my dumb-face replies with meaningful ones. I was finding happiness in my everyday struggles rather than struggling every day to find happiness. I was becoming comfortable in my own skin. I was a born-again human!

They woke me up after their courtship of confusion, and we got back to Paula's summer home before sundown. It was time for *mate*, the quintessential Argentinean tradition. Paula told us about the origins of the tradition and how we were not allowed to say "no, thank you," and must keep drinking the herbal tea until the host stopped drinking. The guitar came out. She started playing "Cluster One." Another diehard Pink Floyd fan! We started singing along to all the Pink Floyd and Bob Marley classics. It was turning out to be a perfect evening.

Paula's uncle and aunt walked in as we were singing "Wish You Were Here."

"*Estamos aqui,*" her aunt announced, as she joined us at the *mate* table. We went around the table with another round of introductions. It took her aunt a minute or two to come out of her shock when I told her about my journey. She showed me the Che pendant she was wearing and told me how much she admired him. She talked about her desire to buy a motorcycle and just go. I was happy to be the guy doing it rather than being one of the millions who just talk about doing it.

The *mate* ritual was over. Paula's uncle and aunt went in and dressed up for a wedding reception in San Luis that they were planning to attend. As Paula's aunt walked out, all dressed up, she asked me whether she could take a picture with me. Wow! I was a celebrity now! A photo session ensued. They offered us a ride back to San Luis in their old VW, and we gladly accepted it. Now that we had a ride back home, we were in no rush. We spent some more time with her grandmother and her cousin discussing our cultures and backgrounds. With their hospitality and affection, they made me feel as if I were a part of their family.

At sundown, we finally squeezed into the VW and headed back to our hostel. Paula's uncle and aunt turned out to be big Bob Marley fans. Her uncle promptly started blasting all his reggae tunes on the old VW system. We were all singing along, as the darkness started eating away every little detail of the endless plains. At the end of the day, it was fun to find a new family and a new home thousands of miles away from my homeland and my adopted home. It was another step in my new life.

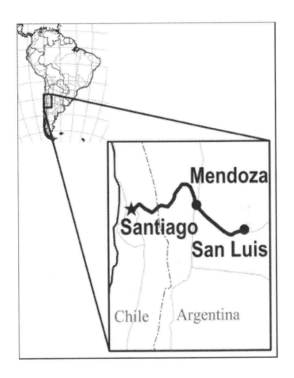

NINE:
You Can't Take India
Out Of An Indian

Mendoza turned out to be a pretty lame affair. Miguel and I made it there in good time and had more than half a day to go around town. The hostel manager had raved a lot about the tours of the vineyards, so we headed straight to Argentina's Napa Valley. Unfortunately, it was a Sunday, the day of *Jesus Maria*. All the vineyards were closed. After three hours of riding around the valley, Miguel finally gave up. We took a quick bite, a short nap, and a shower. Nightlife! Again *Jesus Maria* was in full control. It was surprising to see Mendoza turn into a ghost town on Sundays. We had been told that it was one of the biggest tourist attractions in western Argentina. But it looked like we had just chosen the wrong day.

We woke up the next day and went shopping for Che T-shirts. It was my last stop in Argentina before crossing back into Chile. So it was time to say good-bye to Miguel. He had taken up a new job in Brazil, and his joining date was a week away. He needed a couple of days to go back to Buenos Aires and pack his stuff and then a few more days to fly back to his hometown. Crossing the border and traveling to Chile had never even crossed his mind. But, after reaching Mendoza, he had started thinking about it. Plus, he didn't know how to ride a bike. He knew that he would never get another chance to do anything crazy like that. Stay? Leave? Stay? Leave? He wasn't even carrying his passport. All he had was his Brazilian national ID. He asked the hostel manager whether he could cross the Argentina-Chile border with his Brazilian ID. The hostel manager said it was worth a shot. He called up his boss-in-waiting in Brazil and tried negotiating ten more days of vacation. When it all worked out, he came back to our room with a huge grin on his face and said, "Let's go, Santiago!" We got into a Net café to check our e-mails before we left Mendoza. We exchanged e-mail addresses to keep in touch. He sent me a short note:

"El Indiano màs loco que conozco, ahhh vos sos el unico que conozco. Ajja."

I opened Google Translate, read the translation, and laughed out loud in the quiet Net café. "The Indian crazier than I know, ahhh you're the only one I know. Ajja."

We started a little after noon. The hostel manager had told us that it was a paved and divided highway all the way to Santiago, two hundred kilometers—four hours, tops. A beautiful turquoise lake up in the Andes added an extra hour. It was getting colder and colder, as we started our ascent toward the border. To make things worse, it started raining when we still had about a thousand meters to climb. With my gloves all wet, it was impossible to handle the winds; even at twenty to thirty kilometers per hour. There were times when I couldn't even feel my fingers. We had to pull over a couple of times to make sure I was not getting frostbite. We finally reached the border at some twenty-five hundred meters above sea level. No wonder it was so cold!

While the road was paved and well maintained, the lines at the immigration counters were long. My paperwork was all in place, and it didn't take me too long to get my passport stamped. But it was a totally different story for Miguel. He had to jump through a lot of hoops before the Chilean authorities were finally convinced that he was not a Brazilian fugitive or a potential immigrant. It took us almost three hours at the border before they finally let us into Chile.

Chile welcomed us with a long tunnel followed by hairpin bends stretching all the way to hell. Luckily, the rains were dying down, and it was getting warmer. But the roads were still wet and slippery. The huge cargo trucks and their wide turns were making it difficult to navigate those hairpin bends. It was such a steep drop that, even in first gear, the truckers had one foot on their brake pedals. As we were passing all those trucks, we could literally smell all those burning brakes. All in all, it was a thrilling ride.

After an hour-long ordeal through those treacherous bends, we finally hit the plains on the other side. A gigantic statue of one of the Native American warrior gods welcomed us back to civilization. With a wide and divided highway, it was fun to cross the hundred-kilometer-per-hour mark as we reached Santiago.

It was past ten o'clock when we found a hostel in Santiago and dumped our wet stuff in the room. The hostel manager was nice enough to share his pizza with us and bend the house rules to give us some Scotch on the rocks. We met a Dutch philosophy major and a French education major, who had gotten there through some exchange programs. They started talking about Theo van Gogh's death and Sarkozy's popularity—while I was wondering when India was going to be rich enough to incorporate these exchange programs into her university curricula! It was fun to see those students in their early twenties stepping out of their countries and experiencing foreign cultures before forming their opinions about the world and life in general. I remember my days as a kid growing up in India. The rigid social structure of India, strange notions about life in America and prejudiced views about Western culture; it caused us to misunderstand the values of the Western world, to claim moral high ground, and to criticize others' policies, while turning a blind eye toward our own flawed policies. The attempts to imitate Western pop culture and the long lines outside the U.S. embassies made it all the more ironic. Yes, you have to travel abroad to appreciate the things you have in your own country. But it's hard to point fingers at yourself without stepping out of your own country and broadening your horizons.

It would be unfair to criticize India without pointing out her strengths, though. For an outsider, visiting India is like smoking that first cigarette. If you look at it superficially, it is a country full of poverty and corruption, a democracy with institutions that are perpetually on the brink of failure. But if you spend enough time in India, you realize that they never collapse. Corruption is so endemic in the system that Indians have accepted it as an inalienable part of their lives. The corruption in India has forced her citizens to be libertarians. Nobody trusts the government. Nobody depends on the government. Nobody wants to deal with the government. There is an "agent" for everything. You don't go to a government employee if you want to deal with the government. You go to your agent.

Even after almost a century of social reforms, the rigid social structure is so entrenched in the Indian psyche that it can suffocate outsiders visiting India. Government-run affirmative action programs have led to more divisions among the various castes. Instead of looking at affirmative action as a stepping stone to move from "reserved" categories to the "open" category, people in "reserved" categories are trying to milk the government for more and more concessions. Instead of trying to move from the oppressed to the liberated category, more and more communities are trying to prove that they are oppressed, so that they can qualify for the government handouts.

Indians pull no punches in praising the rise of Obama, and they point out that the minorities of India have risen all the way to the presidency. But they wake up the next day and start gossiping and spreading rumors about the single mother and her kid down the street. They yearn for their own Obama, but they fail to realize that meritocracy comes before an Obama. While certain sections of the society feel that they are entitled to social privileges, other sections have to work twice as hard to claim the same privileges. If there is no level playing field, there is no Obama.

In spite of all these imperfections, if you inhale it right and hold the smoke for a while, you'll be addicted to India. People who visit India rarely go back home with mixed feelings. They either really love India or really hate India.

According to one urban legend in India, a Western official once visited India to learn more about her vast railway network. After spending a few weeks studying the network, the official confessed, "Before visiting India, I was a nonbeliever. But there is no way this system can work without a God!"

A friend of mine had never been to Asia. She had traveled outside the United States, but she had only visited developed western European countries. When she visited India, she spent most of her time at her friend's house, which was on a pretty busy intersection. There were no lights and no stop signs. For the first time in her life, she saw entire families riding on motorcycles—husband, wife, and two kids. She spent hours sitting on the deck observing the traffic at the intersection. She thought she would witness at least one accident. There were none.

India defines functioning chaos. She is almost like a bad experiment with a happy ending. Every state has its own culture, its own language, its own food, its own dance form; it's like putting all the European countries together to form one big country. Who wants to do that? But that's where the beauty of India lies—in her diversity. Unlike the diversity of America, which has an "Imported from" label, the diversity of India is homegrown. And, as improbable as it sounds, the combination of the diversity, the Hindu philosophy, the poverty, the non-functioning systems, and a host of other factors somehow puts a smile on every Indian's face. If there is one common thread that holds all Indians together, it is contentment. They all have their own fights, their own struggles, and their own grievances. But at the end of the day, they are happy with their lives.

The contentment of Indians is almost contagious. It makes you wonder whether prosperity, meritocracy or functioning institutions have anything to do with happiness. I remember my first few months in the United States. As a teenager growing up in India, I had heard about the famous "system" of America. My parents used to talk about it all the time. But being a part of that system was a whole new experience. I saw clean roads. Majestic expressways. Suburban mansions. Twenty-four hour electricity and running water. The impressive 9-1-1 system. Government employees showing up on time. People standing in lines and actually taking driving tests to get their driver's licenses.

And my personal favorite—the stop sign. It's nothing less than the eighth wonder for an Indian. Are these guys out of their minds? They don't even honk to negotiate a four-way stop sign. This would never work in India! If there is heaven on earth, this is it! The rule of law reigns supreme. And following the system becomes your first and foremost duty.

As the initial shock and awe subsided, I started making new friends in heaven. And that's when all heaven broke loose. The land where everything works has given the people an aura of independence. Asking your friends for help is a sign of weakness. If your friend helps you out, you try to put a price tag on it. Asking your parents for help is a sign of incompetence. If you move back to your parents' house, your friends and family start looking down on you. Wait a minute. I thought we were social animals. I thought we needed each other to survive!

I remember the first time I met an American girl whose parents were divorced. An "Oh, I'm sorry" inadvertently slipped out of my mouth. Growing up in a middle-class family in India, none of my friends—literally, none—were children of divorced parents. There was an occasional friend who had lost his father or mother. But divorce was almost unheard of. And it was not as if I didn't have enough friends. If anything, my parents had always complained about me having too many friends and devoting too much time to them. But the social stigma of divorce was so entrenched in my mind that, to me, it was almost like the death of your parent. For better or worse, it was considered something to feel sorry about.

It didn't take me too long to learn to respond with a blank face, or just an "Oh," or an extended "Hmmmmm …," when someone said his or her parents were divorced. Every other person I was meeting had parents who had separated, divorced, or remarried. It almost felt like commitment and sacrifice for the sake of your kids were just a bunch of weasel words.

For Indians migrating to the United States, there is a certain cognitive dissonance in the way American society works. We fall in love with the freedom of expression, the structured life, and the wide range of opportunities that the society offers. But, even after spending decades in the States, we find it difficult to reconcile that with a sense of erosion of the human bond.

The societies of India and America almost seem like two

sides of the same coin. Both are democracies. One believes in the supremacy of the system over everything else. Friends, family, neighbors—everything "human" takes a backseat. Everyone is playing his or her part to make it a beautiful and functioning society. The other believes in the supremacy of the human bond. Every rule and every law can be bent to help your friends, family, or neighbors. The system may not be efficient, but it's still beautiful and functioning. One is full of social animals on the national level, and the other is full of social animals at the individual level. You would think that the rule of law is the key to happiness. Nice try!

The Indian immigrant to the United States is perpetually caught in the crossfire between the system and the society: laws and friends, individualism and family values, personal ambition and the loneliness of suburban life. Every once in a while, he pulls that coin out of his mind, tosses it up, and sees it land with the Indian side facing up. He looks back at the Indian society with the romantic fondness of lost love. He has his doubts about going back to the Indian life, but he loves to talk about it. Call up a few Indian friends, pour some drinks, play some Indian music, and enjoy the Indian high.

As he wakes up with a hangover, he quietly slips the coin back into his mind and goes to work. *Good-bye my sweetheart, hello nine to five!*

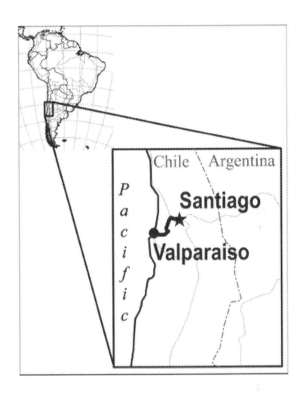

TEN:
An Old Friend

Miguel and I spent the next day in the tourist district of Santiago. My travel bible told me that the British had managed the city in pre-independence Chile. Sure enough, they've left their mark by building clock towers between the imposing government buildings and the surrounding plazas built by the Spaniards. The downtown financial district was full of old buildings with huge rocky façades sharing the stage with shiny glass-clad buildings. Downtown Santiago almost felt like Manhattan "light," with a Spanish twist—a good cocktail, right?

We hit the *mercado central* for some late-afternoon shots of *pisco* sours and fresh fish. After a heavy lunch, it was time to climb up the beautiful Santa Lucia mountain. It was the Bandra bandstand of Santiago. In a largely conservative Catholic country, Santa Lucia was a refuge for young couples to skip classes and find a quiet corner to express their love for each other. Miguel and I clearly did not belong there—unless we were holding hands, of course—but we did not want to miss out on the Victorian fountains, the ornate gardens surrounding them, and the breathtaking view of the city from the top of the mountain.

The sun had started its descent, and it was time for me to leave for Viña del Mar. I had called up Maria, my former colleague, and told her that I would get there by eight in the evening. I was not sure whether showing up at her doorstep with some Brazilian amigo I had met in Córdoba was a good idea. But, I guess Miguel got the hint. He decided to stay in Santiago for an extra day and meet the *Chileno* that we had met in Córdoba. I packed my bags, filled up the tank, and started riding west to play catch-up with the sinking sun.

It was a great two-hour ride through some gentle mountains and vineyards. This was the wine center of Chile, with balmy temperatures and the grapes smiling all year round. It was a beautiful ride: a winding road, ranges of mountains carefully tucked under a blanket of vineyards, and the setting sun busy painting the heavens. My mind was jogging backward and replaying the fun memories of the time when we were colleagues. Good stuff!

I realized that, for the first time in my life, I had spent more than three weeks without meeting or even talking to any of my family members or friends! It had been a week since I had picked up Miguel from Córdoba. But, with the language barrier, it was difficult to share my stories or my excitement with him.

It's funny what bumping into strangers for three weeks

can do to you. You start craving for something old, something familiar, something that will act as a grounding force. It's an educational experience. It teaches you how important the world around you is: the nosy neighbor, the tree in your back-yard, the bartender at your neighborhood bar, the chair sitting in your front porch, your annoying boss, the girl in your office building whom you only exchange smiles with, the custodian minding his own business, the fancy car in your parking lot, the guy working at your coffee shop, friends who call too often, friends who don't call often, friends who never call.

Life is just a bunch of random events. Yet we all strive for that illusion of grounding: in our neighborhood, com-munity, city, nation, cast, creed, religion, or race. And we use these man-made excuses to call ourselves something more than animals. This illusion of grounding feeds an illusion of being better than animals.

Wow, wow, wow! Hold on, buddy! We're just an hour away from our old friend. There's no need to get all philosophical. We have better things to think about!

As I approached Valparaiso, the city lights were giving a standing ovation to the artist on the horizon for his last paint-ing of the day. I got my first glimpse of the bay, as I started my final descent toward Valparaiso's sister city, Viña del Mar. It feels as if nature has carved out an amphitheater for people to sit back, relax, and enjoy the view of the grand Pacific.

I pulled over in Viña del Mar and opened up my map to figure out how to get to my friend's house. A family walking along the sidewalk noticed me as I was juggling my helmet, gloves, and *The Lonely Planet*. They stopped by, helped me with the directions, asked where I was from, did their ritualistic "Oh, Hindu," and walked away.

I reached Maria's house, a gated community with mani-cured lawns and a small, beautiful garden. As I met her in the parking lot, I noticed that I was way more excited than her about meeting again. She was in her hometown, and she probably had tons of other things going on in her life. But I was in a foreign land. Other than bumping into strangers, there was nothing going on in my life. Plus, she was the only person I knew in Chile. After wandering around for a month or so, I had finally met someone to share my stories with.

First things first, home cooked food! I took a quick shower and joined her dad for dinner. Her mom, who understood English but didn't feel confident enough to speak, served us a nice eggs and steak dinner and joined the audience. Her dad had traveled a fair bit and knew some English. They were both successful doctors. She was a graceful lady, a smart, worldly-wise woman with her own mind. He was the patriarch, full of chivalry and sarcasm. As I started talking about my trip, they couldn't understand why anyone would do anything stupid like that. I wish I had a good answer to that!

The Motorcycle Diaries doesn't cut it for everyone. Was Che just a guerilla warrior bordering on lunacy? Or was he a truly transformative and revolutionary figure? The jury is still out for a lot of South Americans.

It took me half a day of lazing around to rest my aching back and neck. It had been a long time since I had enjoyed sleeping on a comfortable bed. The next day, I realized that I was in a pretty upscale neighborhood of Viña del Mar, as I took in the surrounding bungalows, the fancy cars, the clean roads, and the beautiful view of the Pacific from her balcony. It was one of those days when you feel like pulling up a reclining chair on the balcony, grabbing a nice novel, and spending the whole day enjoying the gentle breeze. The clouds were playing spoilsport, but my friend told me that the mornings in Viña del Mar were always cloudy.

It was tourist time. Maria's brother, a daytime engineering student and a nighttime car-freak mechanic, joined us on our tour of the twin cities. We started from the northern tip of the bay. We enjoyed Chilean empanadas on the seashore with a great view of the sand dunes. We worked our way down along the coast, stopping at a few beaches on the way. The other end of the bay was full of all the tourist attractions: the promenade, the huge mansions for the police chief and the president of Chile, the casino on the waterfront, the fancy stores, and the upscale restaurant overlooking the Pacific. We spent the whole day enjoying the scenery.

It was late in the afternoon, and we were walking down the promenade, when the sun started peeking out of the clouds. Her brother had to get back to work. So we dropped him back home and headed to her *Universidad de Valparaiso* lab. Her new boss was a Cornell graduate who had married a Chilean guy and moved to Valparaiso. I guess it had been a while since her boss had met an American or, for that matter, an English-speaking person. We started with life in Chile and America and moved to music. She was a well-accomplished guitar player. As a graduate student, she had bumped into a group of Indian students and formed an Indian classical music group at Cornell. I had never imagined discussing Indian classical music with an American neuroscience professor settled in Chile. But there I was, nodding away, as we started discussing the intricacies of the beats and *ragas* of Indian classical music. She told me she had realized how primitive the beats in western music are when she learned about Indian beat cycles of twelve and a half, or seventeen, or pretty much any number you can imagine. We talked about *tabla* being one of the very few percussion instruments in the world that produces harmonic overtones, the source of its rich sound. The complicated structures of the *ragas*, the time of day and season associated with each *raga*—there was no end in sight to the conversation. The depth of her knowledge was just incredible! As I was listening to her, I realized that we don't need a salesman for the rich and valuable traditions of our cultures. They sell themselves.

As I was busy discussing music with her boss, Maria was busy bribing her lab mates into joining us for drinks. Her friends came onboard as soon as she agreed to pay for their drinks. Free alcohol is the opium of grad students!

It was early in the evening, and the sun was out. We drove up the steep hills to get a full view of the harbor. With its chaotic traffic, small alleys full of graffiti, and rough-and-tumble neighborhoods, Valparaiso felt like the rebellious brother of its high-maintenance sister city Viña del Mar. The valley was the San Francisco of South America, with all the artists and students painting the walls of Valparaiso, and the rich people surrounding themselves with the beautiful gardens and plush neighborhoods of Viña del Mar.

We took a ceremonial break to take pictures of the bay and headed to a dingy bar famous among students for its cheap drinks and good music. As the *piscolas* started flowing, we started talking about our times as colleagues back in the States. Our boss-bashing gave way to their discussion about life as a woman in Chile. These were all women in their late twenties: fiercely independent, devoting their productive years to science, defying all social norms, and trying to claim their rightful place in a historically male-chauvinistic culture. The election of Bachelet as their first woman president had given a big boost to their feminist aspirations.

When the discussion moved to their search for the right guy, they mentioned that it was difficult to find the right one. They were looking for well-educated, chivalrous guys who would respect their independence and be loyal to them. That's a tall order for the clueless and rather primitive guy species! Pursuit of sex, money, and power define a guy's world. Pick one, pick two, or pick all three, and start working. Guys spend their entire adult lives going in circles. As they say, first love is the last illness of their childhood. In come indulgence and greed. Chivalry, loyalty, sacrifice, moderation—what's that all about?

Where are these smart, educated Chilean women going to find their dream men? It must be tough to be a feminist woman in this world.

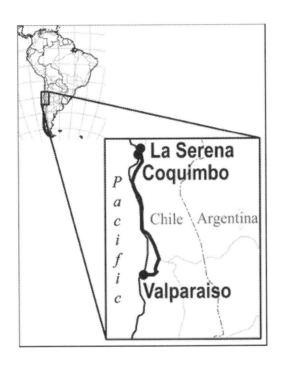

ELEVEN:
Old New Friends?
New Old Friends?

I woke up to another cloudy morning, with mixed feelings about heading north. With only one north-south highway, I had to take the same road back to Cuzco. I was not on uncharted territory anymore. But the first stop on my way back was La Serena, which meant Juan, the mechanic, Alex, the bar manager, and Diego, the bar manager's friend. I was looking forward to meeting my old new friends again. It would be another opportunity to thank Juan for his services. But before that, I had to hunt Miguel down.

It was well past noon when I finally found the hostel that Miguel was staying in. We left the beautiful green mountains of the Valparaiso Bay and embraced the rugged brown hills around La Serena. As we entered the city, the street lights had started replacing the twilight. Showers, washing clothes, e-mails, cheap food—then we were ready to hit the bars. First stop—our good old bar! They were surprised to see "Appu" come back to their bar. The only other Indian they knew was Appu from *The Simpsons*. So that was my new nickname. I had to follow it up with "Thank you, come again."

My savior Juan walked in a few minutes after we did. I could tell from his face that he had not expected to bump into me again. I bought him a couple of drinks and I started narrating my story. I thanked Juan for all his help and advice. If he hadn't helped me with the chain, my bike would've broken down somewhere in the Andes, in the freezing cold, with bone-chilling winds. I would've been miles away from civilization, on narrow dirt roads, with no place to pitch a tent. It would not have been pretty!

We slowly shifted our focus to a couple of local girls at the bar—a med school student and her elder sister, who was getting a masters in English literature. It was fun to meet some local girls who spoke English. After a few more drinks, the girls were ready to hit the dance floor. They said they were headed to an underground gay bar because the music was better there. It was almost three in the morning. Gay bar? Three in the morning? Strange? Safe? Unsafe? The club was just a few blocks away. There was nothing to lose. We walked into a place that looked like a regular residential structure and, after paying them some extra cash, walked into the club. The narrow, barely lit corridor gave way to a huge hall with speakers shouting at the crowd, and the crowd returning the favor.

A staring war broke out as soon as we walked into the bar, gays and lesbians on one side and the two "couples" on the other side. It was not as if I had never met gay people before. In fact, I have some friends who are gay. Unfortunately, I did not know what the code of conduct was for straight men walking into a gay bar in Chile. I just kept staring back, with a clueless look on my face. Should we start dancing with the girls, and attract more what-are-you-doing-here stares? Or should we just stand on the sidelines, and attract the exotic-gay stares? The choice was clear. We got drinks for everyone and started dancing.

It took us a while to realize that the reason for all the screaming and shouting was the special event unfolding on a distant stage. It is hard to describe the event in words. I have a limited vocabulary when it comes to such events. But it looked like some sort of a drag-queen fashion show. It was a headgear competition of sorts, where the designers had largely ignored the rest of the body. I guess the challenge for the designers was to make the crowd focus on the headgear. The designers had failed miserably, but no one was complaining.

We left the club around five in the morning and headed straight to the taxi stand to drop the girls off. The usually busy streets of La Serena were eerily quiet and deserted. A couple of local guys started following us and making passes at the two girls. We picked up our pace a little bit. We were trying to ignore them and pretend that we were locals. It was not going to work, but that was our best shot. I was walking with the elder sister, and I noticed a worried look on her face. I had no idea what the two guys were looking for. I knew I was looking like a foreigner there. Were they trying to rob us, or just following us to see how we would react? Did they have guns? We turned back to check if her younger sister and Miguel were all right. I was totally shocked when I saw Miguel fighting with one of those guys. He had pulled up a long stick or rod from somewhere and he was whacking one of the guys, right there in the central square. *Damn, what should I do now?*

I looked around; I saw only street lights and us. As I rushed to the square, one of the guys started running away. That was interesting! But Miguel didn't want to let the other guy go. It almost looked like he wanted to whack the guy to death. I loosened his grip on the poor guy, who ran away. Miguel was still furious and wanted to chase him down. I didn't know what to say to calm him down. I was just busy stopping him from chasing the local boy.

The girls walked in and started talking to him, as I started dragging him toward the taxi stand. We were barely a block away from the square when we noticed the two guys and a bunch of their friends chasing us. *Ahhh*. I realized why the other guy had run away earlier. Luckily, we were not too far from our bar. The doors were shut, but through the cracks in the doors, we could see the staff busy doing the daily chores. We went straight to the seven-foot-tall bouncer guarding the side door. My *Español* vocabulary—*vamos, maneje, bien, comer, claro, servicio, por favor, moto, mucho gusto, habitación, ron, comprendo, más lento, tomer, perdón, carne, puedo, bueno, ayer, mañana, pescado, carratera, gracias, izquierda, derecha, derecho*—was clearly not enough to describe what had just happened. Miguel told the bouncer about the incident and pointed to the guys chasing us. The bouncer let us in and confronted the guys. From behind closed doors, I was trying to follow their conversation. I didn't understand a word, but it took the bouncer fifteen or twenty minutes to straighten things out with the guys following us and send them back. He walked in and told us that it was safe to go back home. The manager was still there, supervising the staff. He rushed out, talked to Miguel and the bouncer, and asked the bouncer to escort us back home.

We all went to the taxi stand and dropped the girls off first. Then we headed off to the hostel. As we were walking back with our bouncer friend, Miguel was using all kinds of animated tones and gestures to describe the event. It looked like he was still pissed off about the whole incident. I took a step back and started following them. Walking down those moonlit gravel roads of La Serena, I started thinking about my new life. My second childhood was firmly behind me. Meeting an old friend, saying good-bye to an old friend without knowing whether I would meet her again, finding a sense of grounding in a foreign country, meeting an interesting girl at a bar and dancing with her, educating myself about an alternate way of life in a foreign culture, inviting stares for being different, attempting to avoid those stares, territory marking and territorial disputes among the male species—it was my second adolescence, all squeezed into twenty-four hours!

*   *   *

The free breakfast was only available till nine in the morning. We had to force ourselves out of the bunk beds to feed our hungry stomachs and water our thirsty brains. Having rested for only three hours, my body was screaming for more. I just wanted to go back to bed. But Miguel dragged me to the beach. Luckily, the beach that we went to was a touristy one with lots of shade. All the restaurants and bars had set up their tables, chairs, and umbrellas along the beach. I chose one of the quiet shadows, laid my towel down, and closed my eyes.

By the time I opened my eyes again, Miguel had managed to make friends with pretty much everyone on the beach—even all the dogs—and collect a huge treasure of rocks and seashells. Where did he get all that enthusiasm from? It almost seemed like he had a secret stash of energy somewhere in his body. As he started showing his treasures to me, he looked like a kid opening up his birthday gifts. Not being a rocks or seashells person, I wondered why he was so excited about collecting them. Yes, a few of them had some strange colors and textures that we generally don't associate with rocks. But they were still rocks! Collecting rocks, stamps, coins, shot glasses—where do all these hobbies come from? It reminded me of a movie scene in which a younger woman was wondering why her new friend, an older man, was addicted to fishing.

The man, a musician in a military band, said that being on the water was like attending a symphony. The ripples on the water. The distant rustling of the leaves. The creaking sounds of the rocking boat. The occasional wave hitting the shore. I doubt that I'll ever go fishing. But it sounds beautiful, right? It is amazing how human minds can find pleasure or beauty in those small details that seem mundane to others. To each his own!

We got back to the hostel after the sunset. The French girl we had met in Santiago had managed to reach La Serena and find our hostel. It was her last weekend of vacation before starting her exchange program. We went out to grab a bite before heading out to the same bar again. A whole day of running around, talking to people, and collecting rocks had finally worn Miguel down. He said he was too tired to go out drinking again. We dropped him off at the hostel and made our way to the bar. After our exploits of the previous night, everyone working there had started to recognize us. The bar manager told us that he was organizing a party the next day to celebrate his birthday. Alcohol and conversation started flowing again. It was three in the morning before we knew it. The bar manager didn't want to take any chances this time. He sent Diego and another friend of his to walk us back to our hostel.

The next morning, it was the French girl's turn to be hung over and tired. She dropped out of our Vicuña plans. Miguel and I had our free breakfast and headed straight to Vicuña and the Elqui valley—the *pisco* valley of Chile. We visited the lush green valley in the middle of the rocky Andes. We walked along the dam watering the whole valley. We ate the local cactus fruits. It was a good old touristy day.

We got back before dark, met the French girl for dinner, and freshened up a bit for the party. Three more German girls staying at our hostel joined us before we left for our bar. A round of drinks at the bar, and we were all ready to head out to the bar manager's crib. It was a colonial building on a mountaintop, with huge wooden doors guarding a broad corridor. After passing a few thinly dressed rooms on either side, we entered the kitchen—a classic bachelor-pad kitchen with a refrigerator, a table, a few chairs, and a countertop full of liquor. The kitchen opened up into an ill-kept backyard with tall wooden walls encroaching on the starry night above. We moved from the guarded conversations about travel and culture to the unguarded conversations about philosophy, life, and love. One of the German girls started talking about her colorful past—the guy who dumped her whom she would still accept in a heartbeat, the guy she had been dating for a few years, the eighty-year-old man she never dated but sends postcards to, and the guy who she was secretly exchanging poems and love letters with. Wow! Men are simple. Pursuit of lust, ecstasy of love, or quiet desperation—men choose one at a time. How do women handle all this emotional chaos? Being smarter than the simpleminded male species—does it come with its own baggage? The emotional jugglery that women are so good at would easily force a man to throw himself off a cliff. And then, I see all these women wanting to match men every step of the way. Really?

While we were digging deeper into ourselves, a friend of the bar manager was busy pursuing his lust. He helped the stumbling French girl out the back door and, after some time, walked her back in. One of the German girls smelt a rat when another friend of the bar manager started walking her out the back door. It was time for us to help her out. I talked to the bar manager and walked out the back door with him. There she was, sitting under a tree with her head firmly rested on her folded knees. She was barely conscious of her surroundings and completely unaware of the beautiful view in front of her—the gentle slope of the mountain trying to stop the Pacific blanket from slipping away. I sat down next to her and started asking her questions. Did she want water? Did she want to go home? Did she feel like throwing up? It was quite clear that she had no idea where she was and what she wanted. Alcohol had worked its magic.

It took us half an hour to pick her up from there and deliver her to the bar manager's room. I checked the time. It was four in the morning. Her bus out of La Serena was at seven in the morning. She was thousands of miles away from her country, on a mission to educate the Chileans about French culture, a few hundred miles away from her destination with her scheduled bus leaving in three hours, surrounded by strangers, drunk to the point of being unconscious, and lying on a bed, oblivious to everything around her!

As she was stumbling around in her dreams, the bar manager slid the Pink Floyd *Live at Pompeii* disk into his DVD player:

> "You lock the door
> And throw away the key
> There's someone in my head
> But it's not me."

*   *   *

Our gentle nudges were not working. It was six in the morning, and we didn't want her to miss her bus. We had to pour a glass of water on her face before she opened her eyes. After a tall glass of tea, we finally managed to make her stand on her legs. But there was no way she was going to walk back home by herself. Forget about walking, she couldn't even maintain her balance for more than a few minutes. Our bouncer friend and I locked our shoulders with hers and started dragging her back to the hostel. We packed her bags, stuffed her into a taxi, reached the bus stop, drained another coffee down her throat, and boarded her onto the seven o'clock bus. *Phew!*

It was eight in the morning when I finally got back to my bed at the hostel. We woke up around noon and went straight to the beach. My plans of leaving La Serena that day were laid to rest when I laid my towel down under the same shade on the same beach. Miguel spent another day collecting shells, playing with children, hitting on girls, and chatting up older people about their lives. We met the German girls for dinner and called it an early night.

The next day, I woke up with the realization that it was time to say good-bye to Miguel. He wanted to come to Iquique with me, but he had realized that there was no way of getting back to Brazil from Iquique in time. So, that was it! We started talking about all the good times we had had while I was packing my bags: the girls we had bumped into, the freezing cold at the border, the Che museum, the beauty of Valparaiso; it was amazing how much we had experienced in just a couple of weeks.

As I was pulling my bike out of the driveway, I was filled with an overwhelming feeling of sadness. I was wondering why I was feeling so sad about saying good-bye to a virtual stranger. Our first meeting in Córdoba had been an accident. Traveling together for a couple of weeks was largely the result of his desire to do something crazy. Our bonding through the stiff language barrier was rather superficial. Our understanding of each other's countries and backgrounds and traditions and histories was minimal. Yet we were both feeling sad about having to say good-bye. He gave me a bear hug before I put on my helmet and offered to take my picture to kill some more time. One hug was not enough for him. So we hugged again before I fired up my engine. It was time to go.

It's amazing how little it takes for us humans to create a lifelong bond—a touch, a smell, a sight, a sound. I sometimes wonder whether we are anything more than these bonds that we create. Our feelings for the people and things that we bump into—is that what defines us? Or is there a higher "me," above and beyond our feelings for the people and things around us? And if my opinions are just a reflection of my past experiences and my reactions to them, I would hate to be a hater. I would prefer to look at the brighter side of things and move forward. What about you?

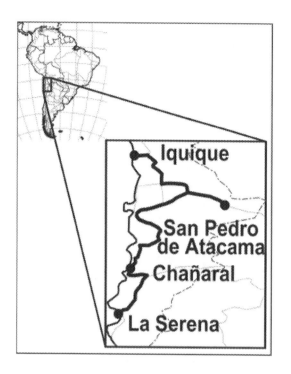

TWELVE:
Three Is Company

After a full twenty-four hours of rest, I was hoping to ride all day and reach Antofagasta. But the heavy lunch at Copiapó slowed me down, and I decided to stop at Chañaral. With no plaza along the thoroughfare, Chañaral was an unusual town. The only decent hotel in town was charging thrice the amount I had been paying elsewhere. I guess it was built to cater to the mining officials who visited the town. I chose the least run-down of the other options, stretched out, took a nap, and started searching for food. After a couple of weeks of having a travel partner, it was strange to be having dinner on my own.

I sent a sad e-mail to Miguel, picked up a sandwich, and came back to the hostel to find some company for dinner. I noticed a couple of guys fixing their own sandwiches in the kitchen and forced myself into the conversation. It didn't take me too long to realize that I had bumped into two of the craziest guys I had ever met in my life.

A Belgian man, a stocky, well-built guy in his forties, was an electrician by profession. He had never worked for more than a couple of years in a row. He would work for a few months, save some money, pick up his bicycle, throw a dart on the map, and travel all over that country on a bicycle. It looked like his dart had hit the very southern tip of South America a few months ago. He had started cycling from Ushuaia, and, in three months, he had worked his way up to Chañaral. That's more than three thousand kilometers!

The Korean guy had left his country in the late '90s during the Asian economic meltdown. He had spent a decade working in some ad agency in New York. He had quit his job and started his journey from the southern tip as well. They had bumped into each other after traveling for more than one thousand kilometers on their own. When they'd met, I guess they realized that their destination, or the lack of it, was taking them in the same direction. So they had decided to travel together for some time. When I asked them what their plans were, they both said that they had about one or two years of bicycling to do before ending their journeys. Future? They hadn't thought about it.

It's hard to keep a straight face when you're talking to these people. *Cycling across a continent? Two or three years? Are they out of their minds?* They made me think about a recent public debate in the United States about whether some innate differences between men and women result in men being overrepresented in science and math. One argument doing the rounds that supported the innate-differences idea noted that the average IQs of men and women were the same. But the spread of the bell-shaped curve of men's IQ is larger than that of women. And that translates into men outnumbering women when it comes to being geniuses and nutcases. It's hard to say objectively whether genius men really outnumber genius women. Throughout the history of mankind, women were kept out of intellectual or academic pursuits. But if you want to know whether crazy men outnumber crazy women, just pick up your bags and spend a month in some remote part of South America or Africa or Asia.

*   *   *

The Belgian electrician started talking about his previous adventures. He had traveled through more than a dozen other countries. He had some fond memories of visiting India in the mid-eighties, when India was still a closed, socialist economy. Starting from the southern tip of Kanyakumari, he had worked his way up along the west coast to bike all the way to Leh. He remembered how he would see a Mercedes Benz standing next to a bullock cart at a stop light, and how almost everything sold in India was made in India. It must have been an interesting sight: a rich Indian businessman in a Mercedes, a Belgian electrician on a bicycle, and a poor farmer riding a bullock cart—all wondering what the other two guys were doing there!

The electrician had seen it all: the pristine and untouched beauty of the southwestern coast, the chaotic cultural melting pot of Mumbai, the royal palaces breaking the monotony of the desert of Rajasthan, the crumbling historic melting pot of Delhi, the police states of Punjab and Jammu and Kashmir, and the rugged Himalayan terrain of Leh. But, on his second visit to India after the year 2000, he was dismayed by the globalization, the long lines in front of the Pizza Hut joints, and the rampant growth of consumerism in India. He said he was glad to see a significant reduction in poverty, but he feared that India was on its way of losing its cultural identity.

We got into a lengthy discussion about how India had been invaded by Central Asian, Middle Eastern, and European powers for five hundred years, and how the Indian culture had managed to survive all those assaults. Will India withstand another cultural assault? It is hard to say, but is India the only victim? With globalization, aren't we all attacking each other's cultures? In the globalized village of today, aren't we headed toward an all-encompassing superculture?

As the discussion moved to other countries, I was amazed by the depth of his knowledge about all the different societies. He may not have had the historic background of all those cultures, but his understanding of the strengths and weaknesses of each of them was mind-boggling. It made me think of how overrated intelligence is in the traditional sense of the word. It is ironic that businessmen and researchers who spend most of their lives in artificially controlled environments behind closed walls get more respect than an electrician who has traveled the whole world. While they are the engines of creation of wealth and betterment of life, they are hardly necessary for survival and reproduction. If a disaster forces all humans to relocate to a small island with limited resources, the Belgian electrician would be the clear winner, by far!

Then again, no points for guessing who would win the evolutionary contest if a hotshot businessman walked into a bar with an electrician. Being intelligent or resourceful like a businessman might have made evolutionary sense when a majority of the population was living in the wild. The surviving population was always blessed with robust health and immunity to disastrous natural events. Now that we've locked ourselves in cubicles and glued ourselves to computers, it would be interesting to see if evolution tilts its balance toward the electrician.

*　　　　*　　　　*

While the Belgian guy was looking to learn more about

other cultures and other countries, the quiet Korean guy was still looking for himself. It was hard to get a good sense of his soul. In the culture of backpackers, everyone is crazy in a monotonically colorful way. And all those colors are always on display. But the Korean was still running around in shades of gray, looking for an opening to break out and show his colors.

Our finger-pointing exercise to decide who was the craziest among us wasn't going anywhere. It was late in the night, and the next day was going to be a long day for all of us. We decided to call it a day.

I woke up early, finished my staple of milk and a few slices of bread, and finished packing my bag around eight in the morning. As I was adjusting the plank to ride my bike down the gigantic stairs, the hostel manager's father walked in and offered to hold it still. Judging by the lines on his face, he was way above the average life expectancy in Chile.

"*De dónde eres?*" the old man asked me as I was putting the plank back.

"*Soy de la India. Estudio en Estados Unidos,*" the robot in me replied.

"*Indiiiiiia,*" screamed the old Chilean man. "*Mahatma Gandhi?*" he asked after a brief pause.

I was not sure whether he was expecting anything more than a "*Sí*" from me. Even if he was, my language was going to fail me again. I walked down the corridor, jumped on my bike, and pulled up my gloves.

"*Estados Unidos, Obama,*" said the old man and pumped his fist in the air. Obama? Why was he so excited about Obama? He hadn't even won the primaries yet. And even if he became the president, would Obama's policies affect an eighty-year-old man running a hostel in Chañaral? Did he even know anything about Obama's foreign policy? Why was an African-American president such a big deal—white man's burden?

I waved at the old man as I turned the accelerator and hit the road. I had not made up my mind about visiting San Pedro de Atacama. It was at least two hundred kilometers out of the way. But every other Chilean had recommended it. And with my early morning start, it was still possible. I skipped lunch and took a break at Calama. I wondered, should I head back to *Ruta Cinco*? Or continue on to San Pedro de Atacama? It was five in the evening. I was only a hundred kilometers from San Pedro de Atacama. It was a no-brainer. After a couple of high-calorie bars, I was back on the road again, fighting the sun. I had only one night in San Pedro, and I had heard a lot about the sunset in San Pedro. I didn't want to miss it.

After a hundred kilometers of nothingness dotted by a couple of abandoned towns, I started descending toward San Pedro de Atacama. It was an amazing sight—a yellow, barren landscape slowly turning brown, and zeroing in on a small green dot. As I approached the town, the shadows were lengthening, and the brown San Pedro de Atacama started glowing in the golden light. I asked the hostel manager for the best sunset spot in town. "*Valle de la Luna,*" he said as he looked at his watch. I asked him whether I was late for the sunset. He said it was pretty tight. I jumped back on my bike and made my way to the Valley of the Moon. It was twenty minutes to sunset when I entered the park and bought the ticket. The park was full of dunes of all shapes and sizes. Wiggly pillars jetted out of the earth at regular intervals. The patchy, white crust of salt sat on top. Yes, I was on the moon. As I was riding to the sunset spot, the setting sun was busy adding its finishing touches to the valley. The golden light and dark shadows were adding to the beauty of the landscape, and, for a change, I was not late for the sunset!

By the time I got back, the city had woken up from its *siesta*. All the small restaurants and bars were flooded with tourists. The lights beaming out of the store windows made the dusty roads look like a patchwork of earthen shades. The central plaza was packed with people enjoying the folk music concert. The signs of commercialization were all over the place, but the locals had taken a lot of efforts to maintain the look and feel of a *pueblo*. I thought about walking around town, but eleven hours of riding had worn me down. After a pit-stop for *carne con arroz*, I was ready to hit the sack.

A beautiful sunny morning woke me up. I treated myself to a glass of milk and a hotdog at the bus-stop. Hotdogs for breakfast! Oh well, it was time to head back to Iquique. I thought about stopping over at Calama for a tour of their famous copper mine, the world's biggest man-made hole on the surface of the earth. They say that talking to the miners in Calama inspired Che to fight for their cause. But, with the tours starting at two in the afternoon, there was no way of taking the tour and then reaching Iquique before dark. The mine tour was out.

It was looking pretty monotonous on the map. I was still hoping to ride along the coast from Tocopilla to Iquique. Unfortunately, a landslide had blocked the entire road. I had to stick to the barren *Ruta Cinco* to get back to Iquique. All in all, just another day of riding through the desert.

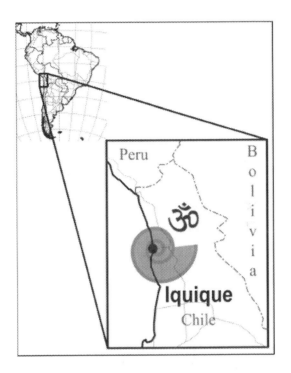

THIRTEEN:
Losing Our Religions

After another long ride, I found myself in the same hostel, along the same beach, and talking to the same manager. The only change was in the faces of the international hippies. There was a German math and philosophy major taking a semester off in Chile; a couple from New Zealand on a round-the-world trip; a lost German teenager traveling through South America for a year, apparently looking for inspiration; a Chilean with a master's in English literature writing a paper on the caste system in Hinduism. There was another German social service major going through a late-twenties crisis; a Native American man adopted by a Belgian family looking for his mother; and yet another German, a chef who had worked on all continents except Antarctica. The Germans were definitely kicking some ass here. An electrical engineer walking along the shores of biophysics and neuroscience was not going to raise any eyebrows here. I ran to the grocery store to pick up a pack of noodles and a can of juice. As I walked into the kitchen, I could smell the whole world on the stove. I gave my humble noodles an ego boost with some parsley and oregano, and settled into the dining area.

The Chilean English literature major was waiting to hear about the caste system from the Hindu horse's mouth. She had had an incredible life, full of trials and tribulations. She was one of six, all raised by her single mother. She had worked hard to get a scholarship in one of the top private schools in Santiago and had majored in English with good grades. With her job as a teacher, she was hoping to save enough to pay for her master's degree. She talked about growing up in Pinochet's shadow, going from a police state to a functioning democracy. She described growing up without a father in a macho culture and trying to lift her family out of poverty. She was struggling to keep her dream alive and hoping to find her knight in shining armor. It was a long list. I was just sitting there, wondering about the non-struggles in my life. Do we call it a struggle and take pride in our achievements? Give it our best shot and leave it to destiny? Or do we believe in the notion that we are just floating around and enjoy life as it comes to us? How do we look at life and why? Is it some sort of indicator of our maturity? Or do we just keep running around in circles? Do we even have a choice? Free will is just another illusion, right?

I started my guided tour of Hinduism with an atheist disclaimer. I shared my thoughts on the ancient *Varna* system, and how it has metamorphosed into the present-day caste system. The *Varna* system reinforces my belief in the laws of statistics and division of labor in a society. The argument that a successful society needs a good balance of thinkers, warriors, traders, and blue-collar workers sounds pretty attractive—at least on paper! But then the system starts going down a slippery slope when the thinkers start claiming that they are somehow better than the others. I am not sure exactly when and how the *Varna* system evolved into the caste system. But the caste system remains the biggest stigma on Hinduism. Denying a person the choice of caste and creating a rank order of castes were probably the biggest follies of Hinduism. As if that were not enough, they came up with a naming convention in which your surname gives away your role and your status in the society. It is ironic that the religion that professes tolerance of other religions discriminates against its own followers. How incongruous is it to divide your own community into "us" and "them"? The more you think about it, more you start believing that humans are just hardwired to break everything down into "us" and "them." The hippies and other fringe elements are left behind to "Imagine."

The packed audience of one Chilean teacher was not giving up. In fact, the whole discussion about castes had worked as an appetizer for her. She wanted the main course of Hinduism now. I warned her that people spend decades understanding the origins and evolution of Hinduism and that my knowledge of Hinduism was cursory, at best. But she was convinced that my understanding was deeper than hers.

So we started our second session with the common refrain of Hinduism that it is not a religion; it's a way of life. In fact, it's a million different ways of life. There is a wide spectrum of things you can say, and do, and believe in, and still call yourself a Hindu. There is no one book that Hindus have to believe in, or follow, to be a "good" Hindu. Yes, they have scriptures, but none of them spell out, say, the Ten Commandments.

As we started discussing *Ramayan* and *Mahabharat*, I started reflecting back on my own religious background. What was it about my upbringing that turned me into an atheist? It was not as if my family were militantly religious and that I was trying to rebel against it. Yes, my grandma was super-religious, and my mom even more so. At times, I find her blind faith amusing. All you have to do is walk in and, with a straight face, tell her that the guy down the street has some mystical powers, or that he can talk to God. She is so naïve and gullible that she would start praying to that person right away. Her life and her belief system are almost enviable—there's no need to waste time on thinking about life, no need to second-guess the existence of God, no need to write books about it. Believing in God is the only road to *moksha*, or nirvana. Who knows, maybe she is right!

She keeps trying, without success, to make me believe in God. But my granddad and my dad have given me the freedom to find my own interpretation of Hinduism. They have always seemed more spiritual than religious, their spirituality almost bordering on agnosticism. Maybe it is because, as doctors, they have seen a lot of injustice in nature—small kids dying of inexplicable diseases and people with healthy lifestyles dying of cruel diseases like cancer. It has probably made them question their belief system. Whatever the reason, I have never seen them too concerned about my atheism. Yes, they are traditionalists. They believe in well-defined roles of men and women in a society. And, to an extent, they buy into the upper-caste/lower-caste arguments that they grew up with. But they have always given us kids the freedom to define our own beliefs and chart our own paths.

So, where does my atheism come from? The more I think about it, the more I realize that it comes from the epics of *Ramayan* and *Mahabharat*. They say Shakespeare was the greatest psychologist ever. I would say it was Vyas, the man who wrote *Ramayan* and *Mahabharat*. These stories, quite literally, chronicle the lives of Hindu gods. Like the scriptures in any other religion, the message is loud and clear—the triumph of good over evil. But, once you start examining closely all the different characters in the stories, you realize that, together, they are a tour de force on human nature. They explore all shades of human grey. Polygamy, polyandry, a test-tube baby, a single parent abandoning her child—you name it. To gain an upper hand in a war, the most truthful god ends up telling a half-truth. One of the greatest gods of Hinduism ends up doubting his wife's character. In a game of "celebrity poker," the good men bet their polyandrous wife against the bad men—and the good men end up losing their wife! When a teacher realizes that one of his students is better than his favorite student, he handicaps the better student so that his favorite student will prevail. The most gifted and generous of the warriors turns out to be the most cursed of them all. The god of gods stoops so low as to rob the best warrior of his most prized possession, his armor.

Then there is *Bhagwatgeeta*. One of the good guys is on the battlefield, getting ready to fight against the bad guys. The supreme god, who embodies and glorifies flirty behavior, is at the wheel. The good guy notices a lot of his family members among the enemy troops. He is facing the age-old quandary of being on the good side and having to fight his family members. What does the supreme god tell him? It is fine to go to war against your family members if you're fighting for justice. Once on a battlefield, it is fine to stray from noble behavior and kill your disarmed enemy who is asking for a time-out. In a nutshell, the *Bhagwatgeeta* recognizes that life is not as black and white as we would like it to be. It is full of trials and tribulations, ethical and moral dilemmas, and choices between two evils—but it is all good as long as you are choosing the lesser of the two evils. None of us, not even gods, are perfect. Lies, deceit, and acts of omission and commission can be justified on a battlefield. Understanding that you are just a small, almost insignificant player in the large scheme of things is important. There are no absolutes when it comes to right and wrong. And there is no way of rooting out all the evil in the world. Rather, evil is just a state of mind. There is a little bit of evil in all of us. Every once in a while, it will pop its head up and threaten our way of life. But then, the sense of common good will always prevail.

There is no need to go to war to experience these ethical dilemmas. Our day-to-day lives are full of such situations. All we have to do is acknowledge that what we consider ethical may not necessarily be ethical for someone else. Just look at the abortion-rights debate. With abundant natural resources and a sparsely populated landmass, Americans have the luxury to debate whether life starts at conception. In China and India, population explosion makes abortion rights a nonissue. For the authoritative Chinese, abortion comes in the form of a government decree. In democratic India, the legalization of abortion is twisted to such an extent that female infanticide has become a major social concern. The current situation is so bad that in some states of India there are only about 850 or so women for 1000 men. So the whole abortion rights debate has shifted to the right toward determining the sex of the fetus. Abortion is fine as long as you are not doing it because it is a girl child.

Think about the age-old "Should I tell?" question. Think about your hardworking immigrant friend struggling to make ends meet. What if she were to walk up to you and ask you to marry her so that she could maintain her legal immigrant status? What if she had fled her home country because she was running away from the tyranny of an oppressive regime, or after divorcing her ex-husband who used to harass her? All she is asking you to do is to stay in the marriage until she becomes a legal immigrant. And if you don't, she'll have to go back to her country and face the oppressive regime. What if you say no and she finds someone else? Do you call the police? And what if she calls you up on the day of the wedding and asks you to be her man of honor for the wedding? What if she asks you to be one of the witnesses to the marriage?

When all is said and done, how do you treat your close

friend after the wedding? Do you show sympathy or pity toward her? Do you behave as if the whole episode had never happened? Or do you accuse her of performing an immoral act and thereby lose the beautiful bond of friendship? If you ask ten different people, you will get ten different sets of answers to the same set of questions. That is the beauty of the human mind. The meaning of life is hidden somewhere in those grey areas. You must learn to put yourself in someone else's shoes and realize that nobody is perfect. That seems to be the central message of Hinduism. That's what makes it attractive.

Then there is the caste system. It almost sounds like a cruel joke on Hinduism, reinforcing its own message that nothing in this world is perfect. Secular humanism, the idea that we don't need to believe in God to be nice to other people, sounds so much more attractive—not because it is perfect, but because that is the direction science is leading us in.

There are at least three interesting lines of investigation that scientists are pursuing to get to the bottom of religiosity. One line of questioning is trying to understand the biological basis of ethical behavior. Scientists have started isolating tiny structures in the brain that play a key role in making decisions that affect our lives and the lives of people around us. It looks as if some of these areas of the brain make decisions based on the emotional value of the available choices. Our love, hatred, disgust, apathy, or sympathy for the available choices guides the emotional aspects of the decision. As a result, people who have enriched our lives in some shape or form get more consideration than those who haven't. And these decisions force us to be nice to people who have helped us out in the past and to return their favors. When these emotional decision areas are screwed up, we don't even think twice before making unethical choices.

The second interesting issue is the fear of the unknown. What is it about a thick rainforest that instills fear in our minds, even if our friend assures us that there are no animals in it? For another example, think about flying. After more than a century of trial and error and fine-tuning, we seem to have achieved as much perfection in flight as we can. Still, we all know people who are scared of flying. And if space tourism becomes affordable tomorrow, how many of us would want to go out into space? Take gambling. Given a 50 percent chance of making more money on a riskier bet, what would you choose? Our lives are full of these choices that expose our fear of the unknown in one way or another.

There may be some evolutionary explanation for risk aversion. If every member of a society starts taking unusually high risks, it can be detrimental to the survival of the species. So, for social animals surviving on the basis of cooperation and division of labor, it might make evolutionary sense for a majority of the individuals to have a healthy fear of the unknown. Evolutionary biologists and neuroscientists have started looking into the biological basis of this phenomenon. For example, it would be fun to explain this mystery in terms of the activation of some part of the brain or the release of some tiny molecules in the brain. Of course, it would be naïve to trivialize religiosity into the fear of the unknown. After all, believing in God gives some people the strength to do things that even a staunch atheist might be afraid of doing. Then again, religious leaders have exploited people's fear of the unknown for as long as religion has been around. Yes, there is more to religiosity than the fear of the unknown. But it is clearly an important piece of the puzzle.

And then there is altruism—the bastion of organized religion, the final frontier of agnosticism and atheism. How is science ever going to explain why some people have an irrepressible desire to give things away for charity, or donate money to nonprofit organizations, or just go volunteer for a good cause? There is no logic behind altruism. That is how the argument goes. But, pretty soon, a combination of neuroeconomics and game theory is going to solve that mystery.

Neuroeconomics tries to understand how we humans make our day-to-day financial decisions. Why do some people always buy the expensive branded goods, while others always shop for bargains without worrying about the brand value? Why are some people obsessed with getting the best deal on the most exotic wine, while others actually feel better about paying extra for the same exotic wine? What is the biological basis of the herd mentality that leads to the buying and selling sprees in the stock markets? Why do we choose a lesser reward today when we are offered double the reward in one or two years? We don't have any clear answers to these questions yet. Neuroeconomics has just started scratching the surface. But the message is loud and clear. We are fundamentally irrational creatures. Even the smartest mathematicians and sharpest economists sometimes find it hard to resist irrational exuberance. Our upbringing, our culture, our surroundings, and our emotional or psychological condition play such important roles in our decision-making that, more often than not, we make decisions that are not logical in the traditional sense of the word.

The whole field of economics is based on the assumption that we are rational human beings. So, naturally, these findings pose a huge challenge to a number of earlier economic theories that were considered gold standards in the field. More importantly, they will also shed some light on altruism. False rumors can force even the most rational of Wall Street traders to go on a selling spree. Then what is so irrational about giving money away to a homeless man without worrying about the return?

Game theory is another field of economics that has raised a lot of eyebrows in the last couple of decades. As the name suggests, the field analyses different strategies of playing a "game," in which the outcome of the game depends on choices made by you, your collaborators, and your competitors. The theory is used a lot these days to design and market new products. What is the current competition to our new product? How would your competitors react to your product? If you want to maximize your profits, regardless of your competitor's response, what strategy should you use? Game theory explores those types of questions.

As you can tell, the math can become pretty complicated. That is not the interesting part. The interesting part of game theory is that sometimes, it comes up with strategies and conclusions that almost sound crazy. Take the prisoner's dilemma, for example. The police round up two suspects and take them to two isolated interrogation rooms. If one of them testifies against the other, and the other guy remains silent, the first one walks away without punishment, and the second gets ten years. If both testify against each other, they each get five years. But if both remain silent, both get away with just six months of jail time.

If your sole purpose is to minimize your jail time, it makes sense to testify against the other guy, regardless of what he is doing. But that kind of selfishness is not always the best solution. In situations like these, not testifying and spending six months in jail benefits everyone. It sounds strange and counterintuitive. But it illustrates the point that sometimes selfish strategies are not the best strategies.

I guess it is way too early to say whether game theory has anything to do with altruism. Still, it is fun to think about it. Maybe all the social animals have evolved to have an innate sense of the common good of the society. Who knows? Such a sense might be important for the survival of the species as a whole. Or maybe our brains have some as-yet-undiscovered structures that are implicitly and unconsciously making these calculations before we make decisions.

Going back to my belief in statistics, maybe there is a nice statistical distribution of people along the "altruism axis"— some bell-shaped curve where we have all the selfish people on one end, the super-altruistic on the other, and then all the rest of us in the middle. We are selfish when we are at a poker table. We are altruistic when we see that homeless guy at the stoplight. We may point out the virtues of tax breaks one day and fight for universal health care the next. Or maybe those brain areas responsible for selfishness and altruism keep turning on and off as we walk through our lives.

So, here we are. Science is trying to understand the biological and evolutionary basis of moral and ethical behavior, the fear of unknown, and altruism. Think about it. If we find out that the biological systems governing these three facets of human behavior are independent of each other, it will help us explain all kinds of interesting personalities. The God-fearing godfather types who, on one hand, indulge in all sorts of unethical acts as a part of their "business," and, on the other hand, give away thousands of dollars to the poor and needy. What about the Bill Gates types, who built their empires on some questionable business practices and, at some point in their lives, pulled the plug on their business lives and devoted the rest of their lives to charitable causes? Or secular humanists, like me, who do not mind breaking the laws of a foreign land to help a struggling artist get from one town to another? Yes, it is a gross oversimplification of a lot of complicated issues. But it is fun to think about it, right?

Alas! The yawns in the audience were telling me that my closing remarks were long overdue. The Chilean girl had spent the entire day knocking things off her list of touristy things around Iquique. And she had just been looking for some insights into Hinduism and the caste system. She had gotten much more than she had asked for. Maybe I had offended her by rambling on about atheism, and she was just trying to be nice to me.

I washed my dishes and hit the sack. As I lay in bed, waiting to fall asleep, I started thinking about my new religious awakening. As a teenager growing up in India, I had never really been exposed to any other religions. Most of our family friends were upper-caste Hindus. Throughout my twelve years of public school and four years of private college, I had only one Muslim, one Sikh, and one Christian friend, and all of them were more acquaintances than friends. The Sikhs to Hindus are what the Polish are to the Europeans and the blondes are to Americans. And with just one or two percent of the population, Christianity rarely entered my conscious perception. Apparently, it was a big deal in the Western world. But it was rather irrelevant in my daily life.

The most intriguing aspect of my first religious awakening was my understanding of Islam. Muslims were never really considered Indians. My parents' generation had lived through the partition of India and the creation of the Islamic Republic of Pakistan. So there was still a lot of resentment over the fact that some Muslims had decided to stay back in India even after they were given their own land. My parents' discussions were always centered on the poor living conditions, low incomes, and lack of education of the Muslims—how they did not want to assimilate with the Indian or Hindu culture; how they wanted to maintain their own identity; how they wanted to enjoy the democracy and economic opportunities in India, and still maintain their loyalty to Pakistan. It all seemed plausible. Everyone thought that it was true. And even if it was not true, there was no way to find out. With only one Muslim acquaintance, there is not much you can do about it.

All the political and social discourse about religion was at the level of adults. It was just fed to kids as the truth. I had no way of interacting with Muslim or Christian kids, asking them innocent questions about their religion, exploring their ideas about God, learning about their daily lives, or talking about their dreams and aspirations. It was just not possible.

That was my childhood. As an adolescent, I remember stepping out of my parents' shadow, gathering my own information through the media, and forming my own opinions. Then again, given the way Pakistan and Indian Muslims were projected in the Indian media, there was no way of imagining that a lot of Pakistanis were just like Indians: looking for a good job, a safe place to live, good education, and a secure future for their kids. To a large section of the media, the Indian Muslim population was just an extension of Pakistan, willing to betray India and execute the orders of Pakistan at the drop of a hat. The daily acts of terrorism in Kashmir and the occasional terrorist attacks in other parts of India just added fuel to the fire. So the media didn't help much in clearing the air.

To add to that, the socialist government of India had mastered the art of doling out favors and freebies to the Muslims. In return, they would vote en masse to re-elect them. There was no serious attempt at reforms that would break the vicious cycle of poverty, lack of education, and alienation of Indian Muslims from the society. So, when a conservative political outfit called them out on Muslim appeasement, my adolescent mind jumped on the bandwagon. This was not because the conservatives had better ideas to assimilate them into the Indian society, but, rather, it was to stop the appeasement of Indian Muslims. In my own little world view, it made sense to hold them accountable for their acts, whatever the acts were.

That was my first religious awakening—looking at the world from the flawless prism of Hinduism. Critical evaluation of Hinduism was unwarranted. All shades of Islam could be painted with one color—anti-Indian. The intellectual capabilities of Sikhs were questionable. Buddhism, where you cannot even kill mosquitoes, was impractical. Other than when they were creating some sporadic uproar over the conversion of poor lower-caste Hindus to Christianity, the Christians were an irrelevant minority who minded their own business. Zoroastrianism was some fringe sect that was fiercely endogamous. And, except for its mention in a World War II chapter in the history book, Judaism was nonexistent. Not much of an awakening, right? Then again, what do you expect in a small town of a million people in central India?

Now, on that uneventful day in a small town in Chile, I was experiencing my second religious awakening. Moving to the United States for graduate studies and traveling through three continents had opened my religious eyes in more ways than one. It had helped me to appreciate the good things about Hinduism and to denounce the bad aspects of it. After sitting in all kinds of campus cafeterias and interacting with students from all over the world, I had learned a lot about other religions. Eavesdropping on the conversations of other college students had made me realize that, as far as their goals and desires were concerned, religion or skin color was almost irrelevant. And this journey? This journey had given me the time to take a deep breath and put all those pieces together.

The choice of secular humanism was another important step in my second life, and my second adolescence. If someone were to put a gun to my head and ask me to choose, I would probably go for Hinduism. Some of the basic tenets of Hinduism have taught me to be my own interpreter of things around me. Hinduism doesn't ask me to follow too many rules and, as long as I don't harm anyone else, it doesn't ask me to fix my personality flaws. But it just doesn't sound relevant anymore. Are all the Hindu gods lying in wait, ready to ambush me? I don't think so. If they are, that's good, too. Once I confront them, I will gladly accept their existence. Until then, I will keep breaking some of those minor laws to help the poor and needy—not because I feel it is my religious duty to help them—nope! But because my brain is irrational in its own way.

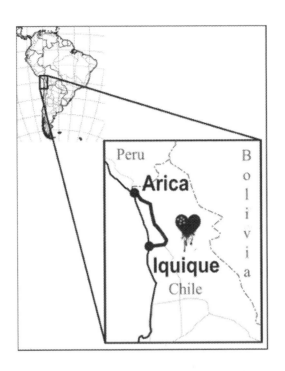

FOURTEEN:
O, Love, Where Art Thou?

I had planned to reach Arica the next day. But after two long days of riding, my body was not in the mood to do it. The beach across the street looked much more tempting, plus, I had a couple of extra days in my itinerary. I was taking the same road back, so there would be no surprises. I decided to extend my stay by another day and walked down to the kitchen for breakfast. With five minutes to go before the end of breakfast time, the hung-over motley crew was busy saving some money on cereal, bagels, and coffee to spend it on alcohol. When backpacking, it's important to keep your priorities straight! I stuffed myself with a good dose of bagels, cheese, and coffee and picked up my towel.

I made a quick stop at the bookshelf in the lounge. Most of the books on the bookshelf were travelogues and classics. I was looking for some easy reading. I spied a Bill Cosby book about aging—a perfect sedative! Two of the Germans, the lost teenager and the social worker, joined me as I was heading out.

"Do you like him?" asked the German social worker as I was reading the preface.

"Who? Bill Cosby?" I asked the obvious question.

"Yes. I don't like his comedy," she said.

Hmmm. I've always thought of him as a legend of wholesome family entertainment. Always emphasizing the importance of family values and decency in public life, he has also made it a point to walk the talk. African-Americans may look at him as the man talking down to them. But it is hard to see why others would not like him.

"I think he's a good comedian," I replied.

"I guess he is overrated," she shot back.

"Well, he is not just a comedian. He's a social worker, like you. He has spent a lot of his time, money, and effort to help African-American people in their struggles. He is an icon for the American people," I said.

The lost teen had finished writing in her diary and was heading to the water. It was just the two of us with the whole day ahead of us. Our conversation moved from comedy to arts to music to culture. It ebbed and flowed through our pasts. What followed was a full day of conversation about life. When I started talking about my educational background, she confessed that the last time she had studied science was in high school. So, I started with her thoughts about the world around her. It didn't take me too long to realize that her ideas about life were incredibly naïve and simplistic, almost childish. If I were having that conversation with someone else, I would have burst into laughter. But the sheer power of innocence to turn "stupid" into "adorable"—amazing!

She was surprisingly candid and forthcoming about her past and present. She was coming out of a serious six-year relationship because of her ex's reluctance to have children. To get away from the mess, she had relocated to Córdoba and thrown herself into a nonprofit child-care project. For reasons that are beyond me, she shared some secrets that were buried in some remote corners of her mind. I was lying there, looking into her eyes and wondering why she was telling me all those things. It's easy to open up to strangers sometimes, isn't it? It would be inappropriate to reveal those secrets to anyone. They say there are some secrets that we are supposed to take to our graves. It's supposed to be our moral or ethical duty. Do we all have secrets, the not-so-embarrassing ones that we never tell anyone? Or am I the only guy keeping those secrets?

The receding waves of the low tide, the bright sun, the balmy temperature, the perfect breeze, a beautiful girl, great conversation—after a long, long time, everything seemed to be in perfect harmony. It was one of those rare moments when you want the whole world to stop, right there! It is hard to call it love, but what we shared was beautiful. They say that love at first sight is nonsense. But it's also true that people who marry their true loves say that it happened at their first meeting. Even psychologists have started saying that people make subconscious decisions about their potential mates in the first fifteen minutes. Whatever it was, it was one of those memorable days in my life.

The stretching shadows and the cool evening breeze reminded us about our stomachs. She was a foodie and wanted to make crêpes for dinner. I just wanted to share the sunset with her. We decided to freshen up, watch the sunset together, and then go to the grocery store for food. I took a quick shower, pulled out the cleanest of my five T-shirts, and walked down the stairs. I was bumming around in the lounge when she walked down wearing a beautiful pink dress with a floral neckline. And there they were, the two German guys, walking down with her. They had spent the whole day sightseeing around Iquique, and now they were back in the hostel. She walked up to me and whispered, "No sunset, sorry" in my ear. Tough luck, buddy! No sunset, no crêpes. The German chef said that he was going to cook some Chinese food for all of us. They were all headed to the *mercado central* for fresh vegetables. Keep walking ...

As I was following the German crew to the *mercado central*, I couldn't help but wonder—the German girl was on a serious six-month backpacking trip. When I pack my bags for a trip like that, I will try to minimize my luggage. But she had somehow managed to squeeze in an evening dress in her backpack. Oh women!

We got back to the hostel and helped the German chef with his preparations. As he started cooking, I walked out to the dining area and picked up the guest book to write something in it. The book was full of notes written in all sorts of languages and scripts from around the world. I decided to open the Hindi account and scribbled a few lines. As I was writing, the German girl walked out of the kitchen and sat next to me.

"That is beautiful," she said, running her hand across my note.

"Do you know Hindi?" I asked rather naïvely.

"Nope. I don't have to know it," she said as she looked up and flashed another smile at me.

As our smiles were fading, she looked up at the surfing trainer sitting in the lounge and said, "You know what, that guy there is dangerous."

Hmmm ... where did that come from? I had noticed him the day before. I had passed him a few times on my way out and I had probably talked to him for five or ten minutes.

Clearly it was not enough for me to form any opinion about him.

"Why? Did he say anything to you?" I asked.

"I haven't talked to him yet," she said.

"Then how do you know?" I followed up.

"Just like I know that you're a good guy," she smiled again.

"How do you know? I could easily be a bad guy. You've known me for less than a day," I said.

"My heart spoke to your heart today." Another smile.

Women, the vibes they get, their perceptive hearts, and the judgments they make—inscrutable!

The Chinese curry and rice was ready. It had been a while since I had had anything other than empanadas and steak. After devoting our first few minutes to uninterrupted indulgence, we started taking turns and telling stories of our lives. They were stories of inspiration, disappointment, love, intrigue, stupidity, despair, triumph, failure, loss—whatever came to our minds. The story that stood out for me was the one that the Belgian told about his search for his real mother. A tallish, brown-eyed, and square-jawed brown man, he learned about his adoption in his mid-twenties. From the day he found out about it, meeting his mother was the only purpose of his life. As he was explaining all the hurdles that he had had to cross to meet his real mother, I almost felt like I had been raised on some other planet. I'd had loving and caring real parents, doting grandparents, a colorful extended family, a protected childhood—everything that I could have ever asked for. There had not been a single unpleasant surprise.

Which is better—having a protected childhood and taking baby steps into the real world or going through emotional trauma earlier in your life? What prepares you better to face the trials and tribulations of life? Knowing that you have a loving family to fall back on—or knowing that the worst is behind you? Does it have anything to do with whether you grow up to look at everything with a cynical eye?

With misty eyes, the Belgian was telling us how he felt when he met his mother for the first time in his life. As much as I would have liked to, I couldn't even put myself in his shoes. Oh well, it was time to drown all our feelings in alcohol and go dancing, South America style! It was almost midnight, and our hostel manager volunteered to take us to one of the fancy clubs in town. He crammed twelve of us into his Jeep and released us at the gates of the club. It was a Wednesday or a Thursday night, but they still had a long line to get in. This was South America!

Standing outside in the line, we could feel the speakers inside screaming the reggaeton tunes. We hit the open deck on the second floor and started sipping our drinks. I looked at my German girl and asked her whether she wanted to dance with me. She lowered her eyes, stared at the floor for a moment, and started talking with others in the crowd. That was interesting! All of a sudden, she was trying to run away from me. She kept her distance from me for the rest of the night, but her eyes couldn't help play hide-and-seek with me. As we were driving back, I was wondering why she was so nervous around me. It was hard to imagine why she would be so scared of me, especially after sharing her life story with me. Or was she just scared of herself, scared of going down the slippery slope that ends in the murky waters of feelings? Whatever it was, it left me as clueless as any other man who has tried to understand women.

It was well past four in the morning when we finally got back to our hostel. I knew that it would be hard for me to go to sleep. Instead of walking back to the hostel, I walked straight to the beach—just me, my sand, and my ocean. I love the oceans. They are always there for us—to hear our stories, to lend us a shoulder, to entertain us, to console us. They take everything in, without throwing anything back at us or even complaining about it. They keep doing it day after day, every day.

Watching the waves, listening to the ocean; it's like life—a slow buildup that breaks into a wave. For a moment, the wave feels like it can conquer the world and change its ways. It bumps into other waves and realizes that there are things around it that can change its course. Then comes the crash. As it hits the shore, it clears all the footprints in the wet sand, leaving behind a clean slate. On its way back, it helps create the next wave and disappears quietly into the belly of the ocean. History repeats itself!

I looked up at the sky above: the smiling stars, the shining moon, the gentle breeze, and the lazy waves. My love was up there somewhere, wandering aimlessly in the night sky. I picked up some smooth beach sand and watched it slip out of my hand. I closed my eyes and looked back at my life. It was like a beautiful meadow, stretched out all the way to the horizon. The crisp air, the soothing green, the serenity and the vastness of the meadow—all were incomplete without the depth of the clear blue skies. There are times when you feel like just staring at it for hours and worry that stepping on it will ruin the beauty of the meadow. There are times when you just want to lie down on the grass and stare at the deep blue sky, reminding yourself of your fleeting existence. There are times when you feel like complaining about that one puffy cloud in the clear blue skies. There are times when you want to keep staring at that one ray peeking out of the dark clouds. And then there are times when you just want to stand in the middle, your arms stretched out, and soak up the tears of heaven. It was just one of those days!

Oh well, it was time to go to bed. In the morning, I got up around eleven, packed my stuff, and hit the road. As I approached the desert, my mind started drifting back to the day before. It had been a magical day. It was reassuring to know that I still had the ability to feel love, or something like it. It was just a small, cautious step, but it was a step in the right direction. It was nowhere near the pushing-yourself-off-the-cliff experience of the first time. Fortunately or unfortunately, there was no free fall this time. But it was beautiful!

As I started heading north through the Atacama, something kept pulling my heart down to Iquique. It took me back to my first love. She had been standing to my left, as the professor introduced himself. I didn't really catch her name when she introduced herself, but there was no rush. It was a semester-long course. We were going to be together for three months.

"The best way to get a Nobel Prize is to work with a Nobel laureate," the professor started his lecture. Nobel Prizes? It was my first day of grad school and I was quite sure that I was in the right room. That announcement, though, was enough for me to tune out of that lecture. There are no prizes for people who find new passions every few years and follow their hearts. And my heart had found a new passion. It was right there, in the left corner of my eye.

What followed was just another story of unrequited love. It was a rather stupid one, actually. It was my turn to lose someone and walk through the four stages of grief. That was the most enlightening and fulfilling journey of my life! For the first time in my life, I was walking through the darkest and the brightest corners of my mind. I was surprised to find out how little it takes to fall in love with someone. It was sad, but also funny to realize that I was so weak. It was beautiful to know that I could love someone more than myself. And it was reassuring to realize that I was every bit as irrational as everyone else around me. Falling in love taught me that the seemingly logical world around us is just an illusion. I knew how irrational my behavior was, but I had no control over it. That's how it's supposed to be, right?

My introduction to love made me think about life in ways that I had never done before. What is it about love that makes us do things that we would never do otherwise? I had to find an answer. I started reading about the science of love. As ironic as it sounds, what I learned was fascinating. Neuroscience suggests that there are circuits in the brain made up of teeny-tiny structures, with funny names like the ventral tegmental nucleus or the caudate nucleus, that govern our behavior when it comes to love and lust. These small structures release chemicals with strange names like dopamine and oxytocin every time we have intercourse or fall in love. And the circuits controlling lust or physical attraction are completely different from those that control love. Yep, you guessed it right. Humans can have physical relationships without ever falling in love with each other. And they can fall in love without even touching each other.

Some recent experiments suggest that even things like your ability to be faithful to your partner may be controlled by these crazy molecules running around in your brain. And here is the real kicker: A brain in love looks like a brain addicted to drugs. Love is the dope grown in nature's own backyard—and it's free!

Even when it comes to our day-to-day lives, it looks like our brains are always looking for a sense of rationality in the world around us. It might just be for evolutionary reasons—survival and reproduction—but our brains start picking up patterns in nature, and we start building our lives around them. As long as the patterns of nature don't change, everything seems to be logical. Our evolutionary instincts even make us fight for predictability and continuity in life. We start forming opinions and making judgments about the world around us. We start loving and hating things. Words like "always" and "never" enter our vocabulary. And then, something unforeseen happens. It puts us in situations that we have never even dreamed of. And that's where the roller-coaster ride begins.

My first love was the first free fall of my roller-coaster. It was a desperate attempt to cling to myself, and I am glad that I failed. It was a beautiful feeling. I realized that I had no idea who I was. I learned how fragile my ideas about myself and my sense of right and wrong were.

Now that I've been there and done that, it's interesting to see people who've fallen in love talk about their strong convictions in other spheres of their lives. It's like a huge circle of rationality. We humans spend our entire lives sitting on the edge of the circle, dumping our ideas into this circle of rational life. And when it comes to people we love, we quickly step out of the circle, indulge in a little bit of irrationality, and climb back onto the fence. We are ready to observe other people's lives and pontificate about morality and rationality. If anything, love has taught me to float around in a moral haze and strengthened my aversion to dogma. Listening to people who I used to avoid, understanding their lives and moral values, analyzing myself rather than judging others—life is way more beautiful when you can take the backseat and watch yourself drive.

*   *   *

I moved from the front seat to the back seat to stretch out my sore back muscles. My body had started complaining after a full month of motorcycle riding. As if that were not enough, the summer sun in the spotless sky was pouring heat into the Atacama Desert. I could feel the sweat trickling down my spine as I approached a *restaurante* and an abandoned *servicio*. I pulled over and started going through my full-body stretching routine. A part of me still wanted to turn around and meet the German girl again and get her phone number or e-mail address or something to keep in touch with her. But I also realized how stupid the whole episode was. Instead of dwelling on the missed opportunity, I started appreciating the beauty of the coincidence.

It's amazing that a fleeting moment of love can add a million clichés to your vocabulary. "If you love somebody, set them free" is easier said than done. But, on that sun-baked afternoon, I felt like I had finally learned how to do it. As I pulled out of the service station, I saw the barren desert embracing the long road. I looked back at the rest area, a small island of shade in the middle of a searing desert—a place to stop by, relax, freshen up, take a deep breath, and hit the road!

As I focused on the road ahead, I started taking stock of my own rebirth. That feeling of meeting someone special, showing your weakness, surprising yourself, learning something new about yourself—I had just relived the whole experience and some more. I had learned to let it go. A strong believer of arranged marriage once told me to fall in love with a woman after marrying her. And then, there is that famous quote, "People marry the ones they love so that they can stop thinking about them." Love, relationships, marriage, sacrifice—to each his own!

*   *   *

The more you delve into the science of lust and love, more you start thinking about the implications of these discoveries on our society. Very few scientific discoveries have had the kind of impact on our thinking about ourselves and the world around us that neuroscientific discoveries will have in the twenty-first century. Galileo challenged the notion that we are the center of the world. Darwin wrote the *Origin of Species*, which suggested that there is nothing special about humans in the animal kingdom. Quantum mechanics announced that the world is not deterministic. When it comes to the future, you can only talk in terms of probabilities. Einstein came along and proved that some unscrupulous thing called the speed of light in vacuum—not time the way we perceive it—is the real universal constant. Space and time are just two sides of the same coin. Pretty soon, neuroscience will have a similar disruptive effect on our society. It will lead to a paramount shift in the way humans think about ethics, religion, morality, and, yes, love.

I am waiting for the day when science will reduce all our

emotions down to a bunch of molecules and chemicals bumping into each other. It'll be interesting to see how our society reacts to it. Would it make us develop means of altering our emotions? Would it turn us into a society of zombies? Would we wake up to a "fog of morality"? It's hard to say where our society will go. But smokers know exactly how each puff is affecting their brains, alcoholics still write poems about their addiction, and I still want to fall in love!

For centuries, war and peace have come to define the duality of man. Science will transform it into the duality between the so-called divine nature of feelings and the dry, unromantic workings of biology.

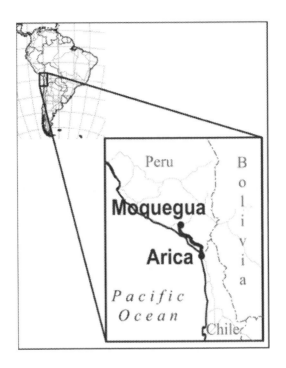

FIFTEEN:
Tying The Knot

It was late in the afternoon when I reached Arica. I went to the same *bidon para combustible* gas station to top up my motorcycle. I was hoping to see the young man again. I had ended up not using the container that he had made me buy, but I still wanted to thank him for warning me. I rode into the gas station and started looking for him, but I couldn't spot him. Somehow, the same old man who had filled my petrol tank a month ago recognized me and came running out of the convenience store.

"*Qué tal?*" he asked me with a wide grin on his face.

"*Recuerdes?*" I asked him rather naïvely.

"*Sí, sí,*" he said with another smile. Apparently, not too many people have done what I was trying to do.

Seeing him again gave me a strange kind of satisfaction. I guess it was a mixture of seeing a familiar face in a foreign land and a feeling of nearing the end of my adventure. The last time I was there, I had barely spoken ten words. But, after a month of traveling, I was a changed man. I asked him about the young man, and he told me that the summer vacation was over and that he was back in school. I started telling him about my journey as I was stretching out. When I was done telling him about the places that I had been to, he told me that I had visited more places in Chile than he had in his entire life. I would have loved to extend the conversation a little more. Unfortunately, the tank was full, my body was stretched out, and it was time to leave.

At the border, there was some confusion about who the official renter and rentee of the motorcycle were. Other than that, the border crossing was pretty uneventful. I was in Tacna before seven in the evening. Sunset was still an hour or two away, and Moquegua wasn't too far from Tacna. By ten o'clock I had found a cheap hostel in Moquegua, parked my *moto* in a stranger's backyard, fed my ever-hungry belly, and crashed in my six-foot-by-three-foot bed. One more day of motorcycle riding to go.

Moquegua was at sea level, and Cuzco was some two to three thousand meters above sea level. It didn't look like a lot on the map, but the hostel manager had told me that it was a winding road and that I could get altitude sickness. I got up early and started around eight in the morning. The skies were clear and the air was crisp. Everything was looking good. I was surprised that I was finishing my journey without any serious hiccups. I fired my engine and started my upward journey to Cuzco. I had barely spent a half hour on the road when the motorcycle struck back. The bike engine died on me. It felt as if I had just jinxed myself.

I pulled the motorcycle over and started inspecting it. Nothing was leaking, and the chain was still mounted. My comprehensive inspection was over in less than a minute. I tried touching the engine and realized that it was too hot. *Should I pour some water?* My two-liter bottle was half full. The engine was so hot, it was like sprinkling water on a bonfire. It was evaporating before even sticking to the engine.

I looked around. I was halfway to the top of the mountain. I was standing in the middle of an *S* turn. The mountain loomed on one side and a huge, empty plane between the two small hills on the other side. There were no gas stations, no rest areas, no villages, no police check posts, and no traffic. *Should I save some water in case of emergency or try to cool the engine and get to the nearest sign of civilization?* I emptied the whole bottle on the engine and tried firing it up again. Nothing. The engine was positively dead. Was it the battery? Did it just run out of oil? I poured a pint of oil in and tried starting it again. Nothing. I wondered whether I should start pushing the motorcycle back to Moquegua. I was at least twenty-five or thirty kilometers away. I was carrying the backpack, the jacket, pants, helmet; pushing it back was the last resort. I wasn't that desperate. It was still early in the morning. *Wait, wait, wait—wait for help.*

For the first half an hour or so, I was trying to be choosy. I was hoping to find a pickup or a semi with enough space in the back to load my motorcycle. Three cars passed in half an hour, and none of them stopped. One of them slowed down and gave me a sympathetic look. He had a bunch of luggage with him. His car was already struggling to keep it all together. There was no way he could've helped.

After that dismal half hour, I was ready for any kind of help. I started waving at every vehicle. Four more cars passed by. Ahhh! Finally, a truck. Damn, it was overflowing with stuff. The driver kept looking at me as he passed me. Slow down, slow down ... a screeching halt. I was not sure how he was going to help me. But he was nice enough to stop, at least. There was hope. I started walking toward the truck. A tall, thin, big-eared, brown-skinned man stepped out of the truck. It looked like he had some sort of rash on his face. It was covered with tiny little bumps. I pulled the dictionary out of my pocket. I was ready to roll!

After ten minutes of conversation, he pulled a rope out of his truck. Tying the motorcycle to the truck with a rope was the only way out. I didn't want to take another chance; I had about forty-eight hours to get back to Cuzco. I didn't want to wait for another truck to come by.

We tied the rope to one of the two suspension rods. I asked him to wait till I got a start. How do we communicate? Screaming was the only way to communicate. What if he couldn't hear me? I told him I would swerve to the driver's side and use some hand gestures. I asked him to keep an eye on his rearview mirror.

As we were going downhill, the truck wasn't really pulling me, so the slope was easy. Then came the first uphill section. That's when the truck started pulling the motorcycle in one direction. I realized my mistake. I should've tied the rope to both the rods of the suspension. *Should I start screaming? Should I wave at him?* We were going uphill. If we had stopped, it would have been hard to get a start on an uphill road. I decided to wait till the next slope. After a five minute yo-yo ride that was pulling me to my right, I started screaming. But my voice was getting washed out by the truck's engine. I steered the motorcycle to the driver's side and waved at him, hoping that he was paying attention. It looked like he was. He pulled over, and we retied the rope around both rods of the suspension. We had balanced the yo-yo, and we were back in business!

After fifteen minutes or so, we hit a police checkpoint and a small hut selling drinks and snacks. The police at the checkpoint were amused, to say the least. Clearly, they had never seen a motorcycle tied to a truck. I hadn't seen it, either! The trucker pulled over. I got down and stretched my whole body. I was surprised that my shoulders and back were still intact after that yo-yo ride. I walked into the hut and saw bottles of Gatorade on the shelf. Heaven! I poured a couple of bottles of ice-cold Gatorade into my system. When the truckers were done drinking water from the tap outside, I took my jacket off and held my head under the running water. The simple pleasures in life!

After resting for a few minutes, I was ready to get back onto the yo-yo ride. By then, I had mastered the art of riding a bike tied to a truck. Using the brakes to reduce the yo-yo impact, steering to the side, using hand gestures—it was turning out to be a fun ride. As we were getting ready to leave, I told the trucker to wait for my shout to start the engine. I refilled my water bottle. I was stashing it into my backpack when, for some reason, the trucker fired the engine and started driving. *What should I do now?* I held the backpack carrier as tightly as I could and started running behind the motorcycle.

"*Para, para, para,*" I started screaming as loudly as I could. After a twenty- or thirty-yard circus, he finally heard me screaming. *Phew!*

He pulled over, I hopped on the motorcycle, and we hit the road again. Another half an hour and we were on the outskirts of Moquegua. He took me to his parking lot and untied the rope. I asked him whether he knew any bike mechanics in town. He said that he wasn't from Moquegua but told me that there was a convenience store a few blocks from the parking lot. He suggested that I go there and ask around. I asked him whether there was a phone in the parking lot. He said there was one in the convenience store.

There were four telephone booths and a store overflowing with all kinds of food. It was a lazy Saturday morning, with people busy buying bread, milk, eggs, and coffee. I walked in and pulled out the rental agency's phone number in Cuzco. The store owner gave me the city code for Cuzco. I dialed the phone and started telling the story to the guy at the rental agency's desk. I asked him whether I could leave the bike in Moquegua and take a bus to Cuzco. My Machu Picchu hike was starting from Cuzco in forty-eight hours. I didn't want to miss it because of a bike failure. But he told me that I would have to bring the bike back. He didn't want me to leave it in Moquegua. He asked me to look around for a mechanic, get the bike fixed, and ride it back to Cuzco. I told him that I would ask around and find out.

I got off the phone and started talking to the owner of the store. He told me that there was a bike mechanic in *el centro*. It was at least three to four kilometers from there. How would we take the bike there? We were both clueless. The owner asked me to wait for another hour. He couldn't leave his store unattended. But he said he would help me out in an hour when someone else was supposed to show up to man the store.

Enter the man of the hour! A short, middle-aged guy with graying hair and an overflowing belly walked in with a shopping bag while I was discussing the problem with the store owner. When the owner said that he would help me out in an hour, I heaved a sigh of relief. And that's when the stranger jumped in.

"*De dónde eres?*" he started.

"*Soy de la India,*" I said.

"*La India! Gandhi,*" he said with a broad smile.

"*No te preoccupe,*" he said in a reassuring tone. For some reason, he had decided to take matters into his own hands. He waved at a cab. We drove straight to the bike mechanic in *el centro*. As we were driving into the city, he told me that he was a small businessman from Ariquipa who visited Moquegua every other weekend. He asked me whether I had enough money. I pulled out my wad of notes and told him that I had enough. But he noticed that I didn't have any change. He asked me to keep the money in my pocket and not take it out. I was a little puzzled by what he was saying, but I just nodded in agreement. *Was he really taking me to the mechanic?*

As we approached *el centro*, I understood why. We were driving through narrow alleys lined with small two- or three-storied buildings staring down at us. We could see all kinds of vehicles—cars, bikes, trucks—parked on both sides of the alleys. The "open road" was barely enough for one car to pass by. And the city center was full of all kinds of stores: supermarkets, hardware stores, garages, convenience stores, fly-infested stores selling meat, phone booths, restaurants, roadside stalls selling hamburgers and hot dogs—you name it. Add the Saturday morning crowd to the mix, and you had a pretty chaotic scene. It would have been stupid to pull out my wad of notes in that mad rush.

My new amigo paid for the cab ride and started explaining the situation to the mechanic. One of his boys picked up his toolkit and joined us on our way back to the parking lot. He changed the battery and tried starting the bike. Nothing. We tried pushing the bike down the slope and hitting second gear. That didn't work, either. The mechanic said that he would have to open the engine to figure out what was wrong with the bike. So we had to take the bike back to the repair shop.

"*Tienes un lana?*" he asked me.

"*Sí,*" I said with a smile. The rope had been my savior earlier in the day.

The first couple of cabs refused to tie the bike to the back of their cabs. They were scared of the *policía*. The third guy obliged. My friend and I jumped in. The poor mechanic was steering a circus tied to the cab.

By the time we made our way back to the repair shop, our circus had managed to attract a dozen or so curious onlookers. As we got down and untied the bike, a couple of them tried to strike up a conversation, but they gave up when they learned that my *Español* was not good enough to discuss bike problems. My bike-problem vocabulary was limited to *cadina buena, aceite no problema, pero moto mal.* There wasn't much they were going to get beyond that.

As I withdrew from the group, they started deliberating on my problems and possible solutions. That whole scene reminded me of India, the way a bunch of onlookers would come together and discuss the problems of a stranger. In the United States, you just call up 9-1-1. You don't "impose" yourself onto other people. So seeing the concern on the faces of those Peruvians was, in a strange way, very satisfying.

I stepped into the convenience store next door and brought some chips to break my note and get some change. My new friend had already paid the cab driver and he was getting ready to leave. I paid him twice the money I owed him. His first instinct was to decline the extra money. But when he realized that I was not budging, he accepted it and gave me a hug. Once again, I was at a loss for words. Where do these people come from? And how do I manage to bump into all these good people all the time?

It took the mechanic half an hour to figure out that the motor had seized. It was gonna take a couple of days and a few hundred dollars to fix it. I gave him the rental agency's phone number, and he told them what was wrong with the bike. When they were done, the guy at the rental agency told me to leave the bike there and ride a bus back to Cuzco. The mechanic helped me negotiate the right fare for the cab ride to the bus stop. He also told me how much I should pay for a bus ride to Ariquipa. *Adios, amigo!*

Bus stop? It was just a big road lined with buses of all shapes, sizes, and colors, and throngs of people running around, looking for a bargain. As I got out of my cab, I was swamped with all kinds of people trying to sell me bus tickets to almost everywhere. I walked away from the crowd and started looking for an office.

"*Ariquipa, Ariquipa, Ariquipa,*" one guy was shouting. "*Quince, quince, quince.*"

"*Quantos para Ariquipa?*" I asked him as he approached me.

"*Quince*," he said as he started dragging me toward the bus.

"*No, treinta, treinta,*" I said as I started resisting him. The mechanic had told me that the ticket shouldn't cost more than *benticinco o treinta. Quince* sounded a little too much. But, as I was heading the other way, I saw him laughing and realized my mistake. I had confused fifteen with fifty. He was asking for fifteen pesos and I had offered him thirty. *Stupid!* At fifteen, it was actually cheaper than the twenty-five-to-thirty range that the mechanic had suggested. It's funny how your brain plays nasty tricks on you sometimes. I had been in South America for five weeks. And my Spanish numbers weren't that bad. But it's easy to screw up on the basics when you are expecting people to rip you off.

"*Quince?*" I turned back immediately and asked him. But it was too late. He had figured out that I didn't know my Spanish numbers.

"*Sí,*" he said as he led me to their office. He gave me a fifteen-peso receipt and charged me twenty-five. When I asked him about it, he said the extra ten pesos were for my luggage. I asked him whether he could give me a receipt for ten pesos. He just ignored my question and pointed toward the bus. Oh well, it was still in the twenty-five-to-thirty-peso range that I was expecting. I didn't pursue it further and made my way to the bus.

As I walked in, the lady sitting next to the door asked me for my receipt. I thought she was the ticket collector. As she was opening the folded receipt, she asked me how much they had charged me. She saw fifteen on the receipt and nodded in approval. I told her that they had given me a fifteen-peso receipt but charged me ten pesos extra. That just ticked her off. She immediately got out of her seat and dragged me back to the office. When we reached the desk, I complained again about the extra ten pesos. The man and woman inside started pretending that we didn't exist. That made the lady with me all the more angry. She started screaming and demanding ten pesos back. Onlookers started pouring in. He tried to ignore us a little more, but he probably realized that he was losing credibility among the locals. After ten minutes of ignoring us, the agency man finally gave me an extra ten pesos back. The lady with me was happy, and we all went back to the bus. Another angel!

Boarding the bus was like walking into a sauna. The bus was soaking up all the summer heat of Moquegua. I stuffed my jacket in the upper storage and grabbed a window seat. I took a deep breath and started thinking about the remains of the day. On that beautiful morning of my second life, I had managed to go a step forward and experience something that I had never experienced in my first life. I had learned how it feels to survive on favors doled out by others. We spend most of our lives under the illusion of free will and being in control of our actions. On that day, I didn't even have that illusion of free will. I was at the mercy of Peruvians. I had given the Peruvians tons of opportunities to rob me, kidnap me, dupe me, or do pretty much anything they wanted to do with me. But I was still alive and kicking. It was a small triumph of people's goodwill over evil.

It was also interesting to appreciate the legacy of Mahatma Gandhi in a country like Peru. Almost all of the Peruvians that I had bumped into had never met an Indian before, but most of them knew Gandhi. His message of peace and nonviolence, more than any other message by any other leader in the history of mankind, reverberates through all the corners of the world. Ironically, that message and that legacy seem to be lost on a majority of Indians today. There was a lot more to his personality. It can't be trivialized into peace and nonviolence. And the freedom struggle of India can't be trivialized into the efforts of one man. But humans have rarely, if ever, seen anyone with

Gandhi's courage of conviction. Like Einstein and Hitler, Gandhi expanded the horizons of our imagination and left a permanent mark on the human race. Oddly enough, the three were contemporaries. I wish I belonged to their generation. To just lock them up in a room and hear them debate ...

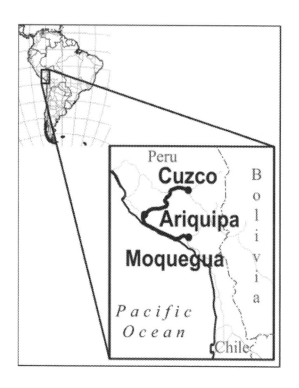

SIXTEEN:
Speak To Me

Three young faces climbed up the stairs and started looking for seats. The scruffy, unshaven face with long, unruly hair sat next to me. It didn't take him too long to figure out that I was a foreigner. We exchanged pleasantries. And I dived straight into my story: where I was from, where I had started my journey and what route I had taken, what I wanted to do after the vacation. Five minutes flat. *Now what?* The bus wasn't done with me. Ariquipa was still three or four hours away. I had to find something to say. His education! He told me that he wanted to get a degree in geology, but he had to quit because he didn't have enough money to finish college. He was working in some Copper mine around Ariquipa.

He asked me about my education. *Hmmm … how do I explain what neuroscience is to a miner in Peru?* I started with "*neurociencia.*" Didn't work. I started sifting through my dictionary to find the Spanish word for the brain. I knew *cabeza,* but that was the head. After five minutes of sign language and broken *Español,* he gave me the word I was looking for.

"*Entiender como el cerebro trabaja.*" That was the best I could do.

"*Ahhhhh!*" he started nodding his head slowly. Woohoo! I had a *Mission Accomplished* smile on my face.

The celebration didn't last too long, though. Pretty soon, my smile was washed away by a flood of questions in *Español.*

"*Más lento, por favor,*" I said for the millionth time. We followed it up with another round of sign language. After ten to fifteen minutes, I finally understood his first question: "Do you know why Jesus can walk on water?"

Damn, that was a pretty rough start! For a moment, I regretted telling him that I was a neuroscience student. All I could do was pull out my dumb face and stare at the roof of the moving bus. Where do I start? Should I tell him that nobody can walk on water? Should I tell him that that topic is not covered in neuroscience? Should I tell him that I'm not religious? I can't use English here. After a minute of silence, he started speaking again. Apparently, a blank stare was an acceptable answer. Maybe it reinforced his idea that God is superhuman.

After one more sign language slugfest, I understood his next question: "How can some people light an object on fire by concentrating on the object?"

This was clearly going in the wrong direction. I asked him whether he was religious. He was a devout Catholic. I told him that I had been born in a Hindu family. But I held off telling him that I was an atheist. For a few minutes, the discussion moved to Hinduism and the multiple gods in that religion. I told him that it's similar to the ancient Greek system, but it looked as if he wasn't comfortable with multiple gods. And when I told him that I was an atheist, he had a puzzled look on his face. I guess it was hard for him to imagine someone not believing in God, especially when they have so many to choose from. But that admission pretty much killed the conversation.

In that awkward moment, I realized how wide the gap was between the cutting edge of science and the day-to-day lives of people. My thoughts drifted back to a small Caribbean island that I had visited a few years ago. We had been on a day-long cruise, visiting all the tiny islands around Union Island. As we approached one of the smaller islands, the tour guide told us that some five hundred people lived on that island. There was no formal government, no police station, and no hospital there. There were no miners, no researchers, no traders, no bureaucrats. The people would go fishing every day, come back to the community, eat, drink, and be happy. How would they react if I told them that I was studying neuroscience? They would probably think that I was really bad at fishing; just bumming around, because I don't know any better; wasting my time on science and not being helpful to the society.

It made me wonder how beautiful their lives were. They didn't have to worry about the stability of their jobs, their next mortgage payment, returning missed calls, checking their investment portfolios, or the vibrating cell phones delivering new e-mails every minute. Sure, science has made us understand how things around us work and why they work the way they work. It has helped us satisfy our curiosity and prolong our lives. But has it made us happier? If anything, the increasingly complex and interconnected world has added to our anxieties. Fear, jealousy, love, loathing, lust, ambition, hatred—even after four hundred years of technological developments, we still live in a Shakespearean society.

Are the island people happy with their lifestyle? What are they curious about? Or do they leave it to God when things are incomprehensible? As a society, have they even developed any concept of God?

The miner broke my chain of thought. He wasn't done with me yet. We started talking about sports. *Fútbol*, cricket, badminton, basketball; that was the easy part. He then turned to something more complicated—at least it sounded like it. He was trying to explain some sort of game that involved animals. He talked about the Sahara desert and the African jungles. Then he talked about kings. The king of the jungle? A lion? I first thought he was talking about hunting. Maybe he was trying to use the hunter-prey analogy to explain it. But, when I used the gun gesture, he said *"No, no, no."*

I gave up. He was still persistent. He took a time-out, came back, and drew a grid on his hand.

"Ocho y ocho," he said as he was pointing in both the directions of the grid. He was talking about chess! Wow! Fifteen minutes of hard work to translate one word. I don't know why, but we both had big smiles on our faces.

It's amazing how we always take language for granted. Evolutionary biologists say that our ability to communicate thoughts and ideas is one of the biggest reasons why humans have come to dominate other animal species. And on that day, I understood why. It made me appreciate all the hard work our ancestors have done to define a set of rules and words to communicate. I didn't even know why he had brought up chess, but we were communicating, in a very primitive way. And it was fun. The amazing beauty of exchanging ideas!

He then asked me whether I was good at chess. He had made some connection between studying the brain, being smart, and being good at chess.

"*Más o menos,*" I said. More or less. Dreamers are not good at chess.

It was my turn now. I started asking questions about his life as a miner. I was a little hesitant about asking him about his salary. But we had established a good rapport by then. I asked him how much he was making, what his rent was, how much he spent on food and drinks, whether he supported his parents, how much vacation he got, what he liked to do on vacation. I realized that he was saving at least a third of his salary, if not more. That sounded like a pretty good deal. I asked him whether he wanted more money.

"*Sí,*" he said emphatically.

What would he do with extra money? He didn't have an answer to that, but it looked like greed had established a firm foothold in this Peruvian's mind. It was just a matter of controlling that greed with some combination of government regulations and market forces. And I was spared the guilt of riding a motorcycle through South America without harboring any intentions of starting a revolution!

The mental exercise of talking to the miner had worn me down. I didn't even realize when I dozed off. The chaos at the Ariquipa bus stop dumped me back into the real world again. I got off the bus and started sailing through the sea of people to claim my bag. As we reached the trunk, I asked the miner whether he had been to Machu Picchu.

"I'd love to go, but it's too expensive for Peruvians," the miner said flatly.

The World Heritage Site, built by their ancestors, was out of reach for a majority of Peruvians. He picked up his bags and disappeared into the chaos with his other friends. I kept looking at him till he disappeared into the crowd. My first real conversation in *Español!*

The lady who had saved me ten pesos tapped on my shoulder and asked me to watch her luggage, as she left to get tickets for Lima. I asked her whether she could help me get a ticket to

Cuzco. She nodded and disappeared. I picked up my backpack and manned her luggage till she came back. She gave me the window number for the Cuzco bus ticket window. I threw myself into the sea of people and started navigating to my Cuzco window. When I reached the ticket counter, the Cuzco bus operator told me that I had two hours to kill. Internet came to my rescue. I e-mailed my family and friends about the towing story, grabbed a bite, got on the bus, and dozed off before the bus left Ariquipa.

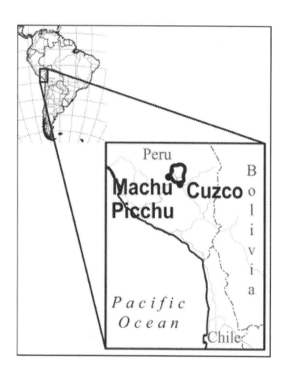

SEVENTEEN:
Jungle Fever

I woke up to the sights and sounds and smells of Cuzco. My motorcycle trip was finally over. But I was excited about starting the Machu Picchu hike the next day. It was going to be my first time hiking through a rainforest. It was a four-day trip: a half-day mountain-bike ride on the first day, fifteen kilometers a day for the next two days, and the steep Machu Picchu hike on the last day. I went to the motorcycle rental agency, returned the jacket, pants and helmet, stuffed myself with some spicy Peruvian food, and hit the sack. I didn't want to be dehydrated the next day!

The tour operator woke me up at five in the morning. First order of business was getting the train ticket for my return journey. Soon after that, I found out that the mountain-bike ride was canceled because of some mudslides along the route. We had to take a bus to our day-one destination. By seven in the morning, we were at the bus stop again. That's where I met our tour guide and my fellow hikers. They were a young American couple, undergraduate students from a small university in the southeast. They had taken a semester off to learn Spanish in Argentina, and they were in Peru for their vacations.

The long bus ride took us through the beautiful countryside around Cuzco and into the mountains covered with rainforests. It was the first time I was seeing the green side of Peru. We spent most of our time introducing ourselves and learning about others. Other than that, it was a pretty uneventful day.

The next three days were pure bliss. The young couple had never gone hiking before. As we sat down for dinner on the first night, I asked them whether they were ready for the trial by fire. They said they were both Division I athletes. The guy was a running back and the girl was a volleyball player. That was reassuring. We spent the rest of the evening talking about our lives, journeys, dreams, aspirations—the usual stuff. They were both liberal arts majors. The guy wanted to join Teach for America after graduating. He was thinking about getting a graduate degree in sports management and was exploring coaching and sports contracting as career options. The girl wasn't so sure about her life.

I started talking about my bumpy ride through academia. When the discussion moved to neuroscience, the girl confessed that she had had a learning disability. She talked about her struggles with the mismanaged treatment and how it had affected her. I followed it up with whatever I knew about the brain and learning disabilities. Pretty soon, their thirst for understanding the mysterious brain was way beyond my knowledge of the small organ. But, sure enough, at the end of my neuroscience sermon, I had found a new convert. It made me wonder why her undergraduate mentor or counselor hadn't talked to her about neuroscience!

They were curious to know why so many Indian and Chinese students excelled in graduate school, while the American students were running away from math and science. We discussed the fierce competition in India and China and how the fear of being left out pushes them to work harder. We talked about how the American government has woven a solid job-security net so that an average American doesn't have to struggle through years of college to survive. They can make a good forty to fifty dollars a day at their neighborhood McDonalds. On the flip side, there's the emphasis on rote learning in India and China. While the Indians and Chinese get excellent grades, very few of them are creative when it comes to independent thinking and research. Good? Bad? That's in the eye of the beholder.

We all turned to our tour guide, who was struggling to follow our conversation. He had his own story. Born and raised in Cuzco, he was one of five. He had graduated with a degree in Incan studies. And he gave us a brief background on the Incans and the Spanish conquest. From the next day on, as he took us through the rainforests, he lectured us on everything from the history of the Incan empire and the Cuzco valley, survival in a rainforest, the local culture and economy, the traditional Incan festivals and ceremonies, to the politics of tourism in the country. We spent two full days hiking through the rainforest, avoiding swamps, jumping across streams, bumping into strange creatures, enjoying the waterfalls, praying to the Incan gods, riding cable cars, chewing cocoa leaves, and walking through landslides. It was a surreal, almost overwhelming experience.

By the end of the second day, the girl had all but given up on hiking. Her blisters weren't helping. But she didn't quit. It was our only chance to see the rural face of Peru. Staying in makeshift motels, meeting the Peruvians from the countryside, and eating in places that resembled roadside stalls reminded me of the rural India where I had spent most of my childhood.

By the time we reached Aguas Caliantes, even a hot shower was as good as heaven. As we were saying good-bye to our tour guide, I paid him a few extra pesos and gave him my English-Spanish phrase book. His English was like my Spanish. So the phrase book had helped us a lot in our conversations. Since he was a tour guide, not knowing English was going to be a bigger handicap for him than me not knowing Spanish. When I gave him my dictionary, he had an ear-to-ear grin on his face. Ah, the joy of giving!

*   *   *

It was the final day of my adventure. I had saved the best for the last. We woke up in the middle of the night and left the hotel before five in the morning. We had to climb up Machu Picchu before ten in the morning to beat the huge non-hiking crowd. We were two thirds of our way up when the sun finally shone on our crazy asses.

We reached the top of the mountain after a good two-to-three hour slog. It was nothing compared to the North Rim of the Grand Canyon. But, after two days of doing fifteen kilometers through the rainforest, we were exhausted. We stood on the cliff overlooking the entire town of Machu Picchu to get a glimpse of the ancient city. Machu Picchu was still sleeping. All we could see was her legs sticking out of the thick blanket of clouds. The sun, her lover, was playing games with her, pulling the blanket from all directions to get a glimpse of her body. She was a shy girl, conscious of her naked body, trying to wrap herself with the clouds. Or maybe she was just unaware of her beauty. The struggle went on for half an hour. She gave way, as the sun finally asserted himself.

Rarely do we experience moments when we are left speechless. An exhausting six-week road trip, a disastrous motorcycle breakdown, two days of toiling through the rainforests, dragging ourselves out of our beds in the middle of the night, the clouds testing our patience and then, a touch of heaven. Guarded by tall, imposing cliffs on all sides, it was a cute little city built out of gray stones. The huge, precisely cut stones, the architecture, the temples, the canals, the lush green lawns, the carefully carved fields on the slopes—the sight of Machu Picchu was just mesmerizing. A city built for five hundred Incans, it now attracted five hundred visitors a day. As our tour guide started his tour of Machu Picchu, he started explaining the significance of some of those structures. He described the Incans' knowledge of the solar and lunar cycles and their understanding of the weather patterns. He told the legend of how the city survived the Spanish assault. It was all adding to the aura of Machu Picchu. As he wound up his guided tour, we hiked up Waina Picchu, the elder brother of Machu Picchu, and started making our way out of the lost city.

As I was tracing my way back to the entrance of Machu Picchu, I noticed a couple of middle-aged ladies looking for a way out. They looked like sisters, and it seemed that the elder sister was in severe pain. The younger one was struggling to carry their purses and help her sister climb down the stairs. I held the elder sister's hand and helped her down the stairs. She told me that they were from the southeastern part of the United States. She was retired, and her younger sister was still active in the health care industry.

It took me about ten minutes to help her climb down the stairs. In those ten minutes, she must have thanked me at least a hundred times for helping her down. And as I was waiting in line at the entrance to get my passport stamped, she asked me whether she could take a picture with me. She said that no one had ever helped her out like that. She wanted something to remember me by—the guy who had helped her down the stairs at Machu Picchu!

A picture for helping someone down the stairs? During my forty days on the road, hundreds of people had helped me out. I had helped a few people out, too. But I had rarely felt the need to take pictures of people helping me out. Neither had the Peruvians or Chileans or the Argentineans that I had helped. I had heard all the clichés about how industrialization has insulated us from ourselves. But that was the first time I was experiencing the deep sense of isolation in someone. As a society, is that where we are all headed? Taking pictures of people who help us?

EIGHTEEN:
Flight Of Fancy

The blisters were killing the American girl, so the American couple decided to take the bus back down to Aguas Caliantes. I was still not done with my hiking spree. I decided to walk down with an Australian who was a part of our group. It was just a couple of extra hours of hiking. We were down in the city by two or three in the afternoon.

It started pouring as we were walking up the steps of our hotel. The train to Ollantaitambo was at seven in the evening. How would I kill four hours? I cleaned up, packed my bag, took a nap, and reached the train station an hour before the departure. It was pouring so hard that stepping out for souvenir shopping was not even an option. I started chatting up the people in the waiting room. A couple of teenage girls from England had taken a semester off to travel through South America. They were from some small town in the Lake District. A few minutes into our conversation, I realized that they were from the same town that I had visited a few years back. I told them about a bar that I had visited in that small town. The bartender had refused to believe that I was of drinking age. She was convinced that I had gotten a fake U.S. driver's license from somewhere. After half an hour of arguments and verification by three other people, she had finally agreed to give me my rum and Coke. The teenagers were not amused. They told me that it was still the only bar in town and that nothing had changed. Now, that was a freaky coincidence!

The American jumped in as I started telling the girls about my trip on a motorcycle. He had a degree in aerospace engineering and had been a part of a couple of successful start-ups. After making enough money, he had decided to take a break and travel through Central and South America, on a motorcycle. *Sweet!* On the last day of my journey, I had finally met someone who was riding a motorcycle by himself. At long last I had met someone who made me feel that I was not crazy. He had started from the southern border of the United States and worked his way through Central America to Peru. He was planning to go down the west coast all the way to the southern tip, and then work his way back up along the east coast. We exchanged contact information and boarded the train. We didn't get a chance to exchange our stories, but, as I've come to know now, my stories sound like fairy tales compared to his adventures.

As I took my seat, a young Canadian guy sat in the seat next to mine. He had just finished the regular Inca Trail. When we started discussing our journeys, he told me that he had left Canada, after finishing college, to visit Australia. As he was traveling through Australia, he had bumped into some small winery in Southern Australia. The owner had offered him a job, and he had decided to stay there for a few years. Both are Commonwealth countries, so getting a work permit was pretty easy, he said. But it was valid only for a few years. He was hoping to get permanent residency by then. When that didn't happen, he decided to go back home to Canada. He had saved up some money, and, on his way back to Canada, he decided to spend some time in South America. He was a surfer, so he was planning to go up the coast to Northwestern Peru and spend a few weeks surfing before going back to Canada.

Why did he choose Australia after finishing college? Had he gone there to find a job? *Nope.* Did he have a degree in viticulture? *Nope.* Did he have a plan for the future? *Nope.* Did he have any goals or ambitions in his life? *Nope.* Was he worried about it? *Nope.* It reminded me of one of my favorite movies, *Forrest Gump.* In the last scene of the movie, a school bus picks up Forrest Gump's son. As the bus is driving away, the wind picks up a feather that was resting peacefully on Mother Earth. The swirling winds start pushing it up, changing its direction every so often, all the way from the Earth to Heaven.

What does having Plan A buy you when you invariably end up shifting to Plan B ... or C, or D—a false sense of security? Ambition? Peace of mind? Some people don't even need plans.

*   *   *

It was my last night in Cuzco. All my fellow Machu Picchu veterans had decided to get together for a drink. I spent a few hours with them, hearing their travel stories and sharing some of mine. The next day, it was time to say good-bye to Peru and start my long journey back home. I stopped by at the motorcycle rental agency to tell the owner about my ordeal with the motorcycle. But the owner wasn't there. As I was waiting for him to show up, a couple of Canadian students walked into the rental agency. They wanted to rent a motorcycle for a day. There was only one problem. They didn't speak *Español*—at all! And the owner's assistant didn't speak a word of English. So I was the official translator in the room. I told them what kind of bikes the rental agency had, what the daily rates were, what the rental policies were. And when I saw them ride away with a motorcycle, I had a big smile on my face.

After waiting for half an hour for the owner, I gave up and grabbed a taxi to the airport. It was time to reflect back on my road trip. It's fun to travel when you can stuff all you really need—a passport, a credit card, a few dollars, and a cell phone—into a small Ziploc, and slide it into your pocket. Except for the motorcycle breakdown, I had not had any major problems. And, thanks to the generous Peruvians, the breakdown had ended up being a memorable experience. I'd gone from the old cultural capital of South America to the new cultural capital and back. I had started out as a baby, crawling around, trying to stand up on my feet. Then, on my last day in Cuzco, I had served as a translator for a couple of Canadians. On the road, I had relived my entire life—a new culture, nervous excitement, happiness, exhilaration, ecstasy, sorrow, loss, miscalculations, confidence, overconfidence, old friendships, new friendships, helplessness, despair, contentment, loneliness, quiet reflection, triumph, disappointment, pity, serendipity, and, above all, hope!

But the flight gods were not done with me yet. They had been waiting for a long time to crush my newfound hope. My first leg was from Cuzco to Lima. As I reached the waiting area at the gate, they welcomed me with a flight-delay announcement. There was some storm or turbulence on the way to Lima. I had an overnight layover in Lima, so I wasn't too concerned about delays, as long as they were getting me to Lima the same day. Soon they announced that the plane that was supposed to fly us to Lima had already left Lima and was on its way to

Cuzco. It was just delayed because of the severe weather conditions. That didn't sound too bad.

As I was browsing through the duty-free shopping windows, they announced that the flight after ours was canceled due to severe weather. *Okay, my flight was still delayed. Not canceled.* For a change, someone else's flight was canceled. I continued window-shopping. After an hour or so, they announced that my flight was delayed indefinitely. I felt like doing the call-my-brother ritual. But I was in Peru.

They said that the pilot flying our plane from Lima to Cuzco had to turn around and go back to Lima because of the storms. I stepped out of the shop and glanced at our gate. It was pandemonium out there. The counter was surrounded by hundreds of people shouting all kinds of things in all kinds of languages. As I walked back to the gate, I saw the hapless airline employees glued to the telephones, pretending that there was someone on the line. After an hour-long shouting match, the passengers finally started receding back to their chairs. There was a time when I would have been a part of the angry crowd. Now, it was fun to just sit back and watch the crowd.

An hour passed ... two hours. No new announcements came. I started looking around for a restaurant or a bar to kill my time. Everything was closed. The airline officials told me that the airport facilities closed around the scheduled departure of the last flight. We were way past that! We couldn't buy food to eat and couldn't buy a book to read. I went back to my seat, stuck my head in *The Lonely Planet*, and started reading some random facts about Bolivia.

After a few more hours, they finally announced that the plane had started its initial descent to Cuzco. We all breathed a sigh of relief. It took half an hour for landing and another half hour for the passengers to disembark. We started boarding about an hour after that announcement. Fifteen minutes, twenty minutes, half an hour went by. We were all strapped up, waiting for the plane to move. But they hadn't closed the door yet. The flight attendants were all running in and out of the plane. There was no word from the captain. Then came the announcement. They asked us to disembark. Why? Nobody had a clue. As we walked back to the waiting area, the airline officials finally started explaining what was going on. They had decided to shuffle the passengers. The people from the canceled flight who had connecting international flights from Lima would be flying out with us. That announcement opened up the next round of the shouting match. After five or six hours of healthy chaos, we were finally on our way to Lima.

The long flight back to America was uneventful. As I was waiting for my domestic connection in Atlanta, I went to the restroom. After spending forty days in South America, I had gotten used to not flushing the toilet paper down the toilet. As soon as I walked into the toilet, I started searching for a trash can. We humans, we're creatures of habit!

I called up my family and friends to tell them that I had returned safely to my adopted home. As I was talking to my parents, they told me about the sense of failure they had felt when I left without telling them about my trip. I can only hope that there is something uplifting in this story that makes them feel better about themselves.

NINETEEN:
Return To Innocence

I got on board my domestic connection and started talking to the man next to me. He was an electrical engineer working in the entertainment and hospitality industry. He said he managed the setting up of audio and video systems at public events and concerts. The company was based in Miami. For the entire duration of the flight, I kept asking him all kinds of questions, and he kept answering them all. When I got off the plane, I realized that he hadn't asked me anything about my life. I couldn't help but think about those Peruvian strangers who had gathered around me while I was getting my motorcycle fixed. Welcome to America!

She's fiercely individualistic. She's full of entrepreneurial spirit. She's a land of self-expression. She gave democratic principles and the illusion of free markets to the world. She's full of contradictions. She believes, somewhat foolishly, in peaceful coexistence of capitalism and patriotism. She spends billions of dollars on therapists and rehab clinics, but doesn't know who the next-door neighbors are. She spends billions of dollars of taxpayer money every other decade bailing out boneheaded economists and businessmen, but she hates the idea of spending tax dollars on guaranteeing decent health care to everyone. She has the best brains and tools of health care at her disposal, but she also has the lowest percentage of people among industrialized nations who have access to them. Her geographical diversity is matched only by the monotony of the chains of restaurants, stores, and hotels. She has somehow managed to balance her misadventures in other countries with successful nation-building exercises. She has arguably the best educational system in the world and the easiest path to make ends meet. Unfortunately, an overwhelming majority of her people end up choosing the latter. She has given us the political party that believes in economic free markets, but tries to impose its religious ideas on others. She is a cultural melting pot unlike any other. But, for better or worse, she's equally robotic when it comes to the work culture.

The rest of the world loves to paint her as a country of ignorant fools. But the level of ignorance in this country doesn't seem to be higher than in any other country in the world. Unfortunately, it is the sole superpower in the world. It's the only country that has the power to shape and reshape the world. And it uses it freely. That places the people of America in a position of higher responsibility. If they are directly affecting the lives of people in other countries, I guess it is their moral responsibility to educate themselves about those countries. It seems the politicians don't want that to happen. It would undermine their ability to manipulate public opinion about foreign affairs.

She boasts a mere two hundred years of existence, and just fifty years of world dominance, but people have the gall to come up with terms like *American civilization*. What about the civilization whose ashes this civilization is built on? They don't even talk about the destroyed civilization. Yes, she is exceptional. The modern democracy of the United States was not established to preserve some religious or cultural identity. Nor was it a historical accident. Rather, it was based on the idea that all men are created equal. But she overplays the exceptionalism of her civilization, which is the folly of every civilization in the history of mankind. She single-handedly brought down *Big Brother* communism, where power was the ultimate weapon of corruption. But she doesn't seem to realize that money is as lethal a weapon of corruption as power is.

Above and beyond all the nations, societies, and cultures, ego seems to be the *Big Daddy* in man's life. It operates through its two stooges, or *Big Brothers*—money and power. The *Big Brothers* in America seem to be smart enough. Until now, they've managed to make Americans believe that they are in charge of their lives. Greed and ambition are good. Moderation and humility are for losers. But when the twin *Big Brothers* of money and power are controlling our lives, it's hard to look past them and come face to face with the *Big Daddy* of ego. Breaking the shackles of *Big Daddy* seems to be the only way to eternal bliss, so—pick up your backpacks and go—go somewhere!

All in all, it's a beautiful country. Her freedom and immense diversity give everyone the opportunity for self-exploration and self-expression. In her quest for becoming the moral authority of the world, she has somehow ended up teaching her citizens to be nonjudgmental. That, in my mind, is her biggest achievement.

*   *   *

After twenty-four hours of drama, my journey had finally come to an end. I got into my car and started driving back home. After a long time, I was again driving something with a backrest, air conditioner, and a seatbelt! It was an amazing feeling. As I sat in the traffic on an exit ramp, I started scanning through the radio channels and tuned in to the hip-hop channel. Snoop Dogg was rapping along. It was a strange feeling of happiness to having a hip-hop channel on my radio. It was nice to come back to my American life. We humans, we're creatures of habit!

After forty long days, I had left the land where every restaurant, store, and hotel would always play the mellow Spanish love songs about *amor* and *corazón*. This was hip-hop nation:
"I'll be gentle
Sentimental
Fucking in a rental
Lincoln Continental."

Express yourself! Push yourself to the extremes, and explore yourself! Don't be afraid to redefine yourself!